MOTHERS

MOTHERS

An Essay on Love and Cruelty

JACQUELINE ROSE

FABER & FABER

First published in 2018
by Faber & Faber Ltd
Bloomsbury House
74–77 Great Russell Street
London WC1B 3DA

Typeset by Faber & Faber Ltd
Printed and bound by CPI Group (UK) Ltd, Croydon CR0 4YY

A CIP record for this book
is available from the British Library

ISBN 978–0–571–33143–7

FSC
www.fsc.org
MIX
Paper from
responsible sources
FSC® C020471

2 4 6 8 10 9 7 5 3

For Lynn Rose
And for Jeanette Stone
With my love

HERMIONE: You gods, look down,
And from your sacred vials pour your graces
Upon my daughter's head!

Shakespeare, *The Winter's Tale*

I suppose that is what we want from our mothers: to maintain the world – and, even if it is a lie, to proceed as though the world could be maintained.

Hisham Matar, *The Return*

Oh God. Is there still mother after death?

Ali Smith, *Autumn*

CONTENTS

OPENING

A simple argument guides this book: that motherhood is, in Western discourse, the place in our culture where we lodge, or rather bury, the reality of our own conflicts, of what it means to be fully human. It is the ultimate scapegoat for our personal and political failings, for everything that is wrong with the world, which it becomes the task – unrealisable, of course – of mothers to repair. To the familiar claim that too much is demanded of mothers, which has been a long-standing feminist plaint, this book will add a further dimension, or question. What are we doing – what aspects of our social arrangements and of our inner lives, what forms of historic injustice, do we turn our backs on, above all, what are we doing *to* mothers – when we expect them to carry the burden of everything that is hardest to contemplate about our society and ourselves? Mothers cannot help but be in touch with the most difficult aspects of any fully lived life. Along with the passion and pleasure, it is the secret knowledge they share. Why on earth should it fall to them to paint things bright and innocent and safe? Running through the book is a central contention: that by making mothers the objects of licensed cruelty, we blind ourselves to the world's iniquities and shut down the portals of the heart. Unless we recognise what we are asking mothers to perform in the world – and for the world – we will continue to tear both the world and mothers to pieces.

I

SOCIAL PUNISHMENT

NOW

On 12 October 2016, *The Sun*'s front-page headline was 'Here for maternity'. According to its report, splashed over half the page, a National Health Service hospital had been used by nine hundred pregnant 'health tourists' in the previous year at a cost to the UK taxpayer of around £4 million in unpaid bills. Officials (unidentified) were quoted as stating that deliveries from non-EU 'mums' accounted for a fifth of all births in St George's Hospital in Tooting, South London. The hospital – read the nation – was being 'deluged', an 'easy target' for 'fixers in Nigeria' who were charging women to use the NHS. The *Sun* leader, entitled 'Unhealthy cost', described the 'scandal' as 'sickening' (the puns on 'unhealthy' and 'sickening' presumably intentional), and railed against the £2 billion 'blown' on 'foreign tourists with no right to free NHS care' each year.

In response to this crisis, the hospital was planning to request ID or proof of asylum from incoming patients in the maternity ward. The article was illustrated with a photo of Bimbo Ayelabola, a Nigerian mother who gave birth to quintuplets by caesarean section at Homerton

University Hospital in 2011 at a cost of '£200,000' to the NHS. Despite the nod to 'fixers in Nigeria', the image of Ayelabola, holding her five babies, had clearly been chosen to reinforce the age-old stereotype of blacks and the poor reproducing irresponsibly and to excess. Abandoned by her wealthy Nigerian husband, *The Sun* wrote, she was believed to be still living in the UK with her children, and no doubt claiming benefits, to which, it was implied, she would not be entitled. The subliminal – or not so subliminal – message of the article was therefore: Get this mother out (the paper just about refrained from suggesting that she should be hunted down). The unions may baulk at medics acting as 'border guards', the leader commented, but the NHS has an 'army' of administrators who need to 'toughen up'. Apparently, a military response was needed to deal with the scheming dereliction of foreign mothers, who were a threat to the nation's values and resources alike. In *The Sun* online (12 October 2016), the article was re-titled 'Up the Bluff', as if these women might not even be pregnant.

Why are these mothers so hated? Why are mothers so often held accountable for the ills of the world, the breakdown in the social fabric, the threat to welfare, to the health of the nation – from the funding crisis in the NHS to the influx of foreigners on our shores? Why are mothers seen as the cause of everything that doesn't work in who we are? We are living in an increasingly fortified world, with walls, concrete and imaginary,

being erected across national boundaries, reinforc-
ing the distinctions between peoples. From all sides,
in Europe and the US, we are accosted by increasingly
shrill voices, telling us that our greatest ethical obligation is to entrench our national and personal borders, to
be unfailingly self-regarding and sure of ourselves. It is
a perfect atmosphere for picking on mothers, for brand-
ing them as uniquely responsible for both securing and
jeopardising this impossible future.

The Sun was not alone in this particular brand of vitriol. A few months later, in January 2017, the *Daily Mail*
headlined its front page: 'One health tourist's £350,000
bill – and you paid!' with reference to another Nigerian mother who had come to the UK to give birth
on the NHS, this time to twins. Inside its pages the
paper reprinted the photo of Ayelabola with her five
babies: 'Haven't we fallen for this before?' The figure
of £350,000 must have been carefully chosen since it
echoes the £350 million that Brexit campaigners had
falsely claimed would, on a weekly basis, revert to the
UK from Europe straight into the coffers of the NHS
(which makes the broken promise somehow these mothers' fault). *The Sun* and the *Daily Mail* are the country's
most right-wing newspapers, but such rhetoric is not
without wider effect. According to charity reports from
across the UK, hundreds of pregnant foreign women
were avoiding antenatal care because they feared being
reported to the Home Office or facing costly medical

bills. One NHS trust has been sending letters to women with complex asylum claims saying that their maternity care will be cancelled if they fail to bring credit cards to pay fees of more than £5,000.[1] It is also worth noting that, without qualification or apology, *The Sun* and *Daily Mail* felt able to issue this onslaught on mothers on the verge, or indeed in the process, of giving birth – the minimal requirement of motherhood, one might say. In this, they are by no means unique. As we will see, tormenting mothers is something of a pastime in the so-called civilised world.

'Here for maternity' echoes the title of the 1953 Fred Zinnemann film *From Here to Eternity*, a phrase which has passed into common parlance in the English-speaking world to evoke a love that will follow its object to the ends of the earth, even if the price is death – the eternity/maternity echo of the *Sun* front page suggests that, without drastic action, we are stuck with this problem, with these mothers, for ever. The film is set in the days before Pearl Harbor. Montgomery Clift plays a boxer who refuses to fight with his army mates and prefers to play the bugle, is subjected to cruel treatment by his captain, and is finally killed during the attack. A sergeant (Burt Lancaster) who befriends the Clift character starts an affair with the captain's wife (Deborah Kerr). The film therefore has all the ingredients for 'locker talk' combined with heterosexual passion. But there is a dark side in relation to mothers. In the novel the film is based on, the captain's wife had a hysterectomy after her unfaithful husband infected her with gonorrhoea. To meet Production Code standards, the film changed this to a miscarriage (there could be no mention of venereal disease). In the film, the husband is still a philanderer, but it is the woman's own body that has failed her, robbing her of the possibility of motherhood. The fact that male sexual licence during the war might be putting potential mothers at risk could not be spoken. In a film that goes some way to exposing the cult of masculinity in the army, motherhood is an aside, like the irritating drip of a tap. At the opposite end from the *Sun* article, although drawing on some of the same degraded impulses, mothers in this film slip in and out – mostly out – of focus. This, I will be suggesting, is a pattern. In modern-day Western culture, mothers are almost invariably the object, either of too much attention or not enough.

The Sun's targeting of foreign mothers came at a time when the image of children without mothers, care or sustenance was at the forefront of the news. Unaccompanied minors were being held in the Calais Jungle, as it came to be known, waiting for the British government to complete the process to allow those who qualify entrance into the UK. In Europe as a whole, there were an estimated 85,000 lone children and young people since the migration crisis began in 2015, roughly one thousand of them in Calais, living 'feral' lives: tents housing up to eighteen children or minors, no mattresses, no heating, no blankets. Several of these minors were killed as they made their bid for freedom in the UK – attaching themselves to the underside of trucks, hiding in refrigerated containers or running into the path of cars they often hoped would drive them to Britain. Despite frequent invocations of the Kindertransport that saved German Jewish children from the Nazi genocide by bringing them to England, the process of admitting these children was painfully slow, stalled by the Conservative government at every turn. In February 2017, the government halted its agreement to resettle three thousand child refugees after just 350 had been allowed entry (a figure subsequently revised to 480, although by July 2017 not one unaccompanied child had entered the UK since the start of the year).[2]

The migration crisis of recent years is by no means confined to Europe. But the Calais debacle has special resonance as a monument to inhumanity in our times. Historically, 'women and children first' has been accepted practice in moments of high risk. But it is one thing to declare this as a principle, quite another to act on it by letting into the country fragile human beings whose glaring vulnerability will stand as a reminder of the utter nonsense, not to speak of the inhumanity, of pretending that we can save ourselves at the cost of everybody else. 'The reality, of course,' commented Bernard Cazeneuve in 2016, when he was French Minister of the Interior, on the breakdown between France and the UK

on how to deal with the crisis, 'is that neither government has chosen to leave people with the right to refugee
status in the cold and the mud – women and children
least of all.' The actions of both governments spoke oth-
erwise. Nor did he seem to register the contradiction
between calling for a humanitarian gesture on the part
of the UK and insisting that, in the longer term, the borders must be made 'impenetrable'.[3]

Where are the mothers of these children? Behind each
and every child there is a story of mothers to be told,
but they rarely get a mention. For the most part, they are
wiped out of the picture. As if a mother's loss, which is
so often the hidden face and precondition of these children's fates, is the truly unbearable torment, too glaring a
testimony to the cruelty of the modern world, and therefore impossible to contemplate (some of these mothers
will have died). One sixteen-year-old boy in the camp,
who had fled the war in Sudan, had not spoken to his
mother for two years. She did not know if he was dead
or alive.[4] A thirteen-year-old simply referred to himself
as 'Mammy's No. 1'.[5] And after being removed from the
Calais camp when it was closed, Samir, seventeen, died of
heart failure in January 2017 at the Taizé reception centre in the Saône-et-Loire department of France not long
after hearing that his application to join his brother in
the UK had been rejected (there have been others – thirty
asylum seekers are buried in the Calais graveyard, many
in graves without names). His mother could not travel

to the funeral. She requested he not be named in full for fear of putting the family in danger from the Sudanese authorities.[6]

These absent, missing mothers are the other face of the pregnant 'health tourists' lambasted by *The Sun* – mothers who are either overlooked completely or are the target of blame, with migration and its miseries being the true story behind both. At the same time, suffering motherhood, a mother bereft of her child, is also a staple of maternal imagos – Niobe lamenting the murder of her fourteen children, killed by jealous gods; and the Pietà, the Virgin Mary grieving the dead Christ, are two of the most well-known examples. But the mother must be noble and her agony redemptive. With the suffering of the whole world etched on her face, she carries and assuages the burden of human misery on behalf of everyone. What the pain of mothers must never expose is a viciously unjust world in a complete mess.

*

Using the agony of mothers to deflect from our awareness of human responsibility for the world has a long history. Lamenting mothers have been and often still are the hallmark image for so-called 'natural' catastrophes such as earthquakes. In these images, mothers are not, like Bimbo Ayelabola, held responsible. Nevertheless, there is a connection, as their misery is being exploited, shoved in the face of the world, so that others will get off scot-free: contractors who put up buildings that collapse, town planners cutting corners to cram as many people as possible into an inhumanly crowded space. For that reason, Bertolt Brecht objected to the Niobe-like faces plastered over newspaper front pages after the Tokyo–Yokohama earthquake of 1923 that killed an estimated 140,000 people. He praised instead, as the only fully political response, a single newspaper photograph depicting a few solid structures standing among the rubble with the headline: 'Steel stood' (only reliably constructed buildings had survived).[7] In earthquakes it is almost invariably the poor who die first, the victims of unscrupulous builders and landlords. And not just in earthquakes, as other disasters have made all too clear: the ongoing tragedy of the hurricanes to have swept the US (New Orleans in August 2005, Haiti in September 2008 and October 2016, Houston in August 2017), and in the UK the Grenfell Tower fire disaster of June 2017. Brecht's point was that looking at steel structures would not make you weep. It would make you think. And then, hopefully, act, organise, demand redress.

Brecht carried his own political point across into the world of mothers. Perhaps my favourite of his plays on this subject is *The Mother* (1932) – less known than *Mother Courage* – in which the mother of the title opposes the war she knows will kill her son. In a key scene, she argues with mothers who are waiting in line to donate their pots and pans for ammunition, in response to a government call announcing it will help to bring the war to an end. She simply points out the obvious – albeit suppressed – fact that their gesture will rather provide the means for the war to continue. This mother is not agonised, even though her son's life is at stake, but focused, stubborn, articulate. She speaks the truth. Her self-appointed role is to strip deceit from the official dross.

In similar vein, Colm Tóibín's novella *The Testament of Mary* (2012) tells the story of the Crucifixion from Mary's point of view, undoing centuries of glorified maternal pain. Tóibín gives to Mary the last, iconoclastic word in relation to the dead Christ: 'I can tell you now, when you say that he redeemed the world, I will say that it was not worth it. It was not worth it.'[8] In the Broadway and London Barbican 2014 production, these are the last lines, spoken by actress Fiona Shaw through her teeth with unerring, barely controlled precision. *The Testament of Mary* also has Mary flee in horror at the sight of her crucified son, which makes the Pietà image, the mother holding and cherishing the dying Christ's body – which is meant somehow to make it all okay – a complete lie.

How often are the mothers of lost soldiers and children given voice? How often is the grief of a mother allowed to wander outside the frame of the requisite pathos? Why is it so hard to listen to such a mother, to dignify her with the story she might have to tell? The Mothers of the Plaza de Mayo in Argentina are famous – they started gathering in 1977 to protest the disappearance of their children under the military regime of 1976 to 1983 (in April 2017, they marked the fortieth anniversary of their protest). In the UK, Doreen Lawrence, mother of Stephen Lawrence, murdered on a London street in 1993, has become a campaigner and activist against race crime and also racism in the Metropolitan Police. She has turned the death of her son into a civic task (that in itself was enough to have her and her husband spied on by undercover police). She is a reminder that political agency and the grief of a mother can coexist – a 1998 painting by Chris Ofili depicts her weeping, with the image of her son in every tear. But mothers who expose misfortune as injustice, to use philosopher Judith Shklar's suggestive formula, by telling the world of the political and social ills behind the death of a child, still struggle to be heard.[9] To put it at its crudest, a mother can suffer, she can be the object of heartfelt empathy, so long as she does not probe or talk too much.

When Gillian Slovo was commissioned by Nicolas Kent to write her verbatim, testimony-based play *Another World: Losing our Children to Islamic State*, performed at the National Theatre in 2016, she chose to make the voices of three mothers – Samira, Yasmin and Geraldine, each one the mother of a child who had gone to fight against Bashar al-Assad in Syria – her central focus. No mothers in the UK would speak to her; in an atmosphere of strong-arm vigilance and heightened racism against Muslims, they felt that they would place themselves at risk, so she spoke to mothers in Molenbeek in Brussels. (This was after the Paris *Charlie Hebdo* attack in January 2015, but before Molenbeek became infamous as a centre for terrorists following the Paris Bataclan attack later that year and the subsequent Brussels attacks in March 2016.)

The play dramatises their history, but it is the mothers' own words that are spoken. These mothers lament the loss of their children: one son dead, one missing and one daughter who chose to remain in Syria after the husband she married in Brussels was killed in combat a matter of weeks after they arrived. They may, as two of them insist, feel they have failed as mothers. But they are also in search of knowledge – it is above all for their failure to know and pre-empt what their children were planning that they castigate themselves. In a world that had become callously indifferent, hostile or meaningless for their children, the mothers are trying to comprehend the choices they made. Two of the mothers, Samira and Geraldine, travel to Syria. Samira goes in search of her daughter Nora – to 'the end of the earth', as Samira puts it: 'wherever you are, I will abandon everything. I will come and get you.' Geraldine, after the death of her son Anis, travels to the Syrian–Turkish border, where she gives money and clothes that belonged to her son to a pregnant woman, one of the refugees huddled on the border. The pregnant woman says she will call her son Anis. The play ends on this. It therefore seizes the familiar tropes – to the ends of the earth, a mother's grief – and gives them a new twist, simply by allowing these women to speak: 'There. That's the mum's story,' is the last line of the play.[10] As if to say, motherhood is part of the polity of nations. Given voice, space and time, motherhood can, and should, be one of the central means through which a historical moment reckons with itself.

Why in modern times is the participation of mothers in political and public life seen as the exception – with the UK appearing to lag behind the rest of Europe, the US and other countries of the world in this regard? Why are mothers not seen as having everything to contribute, by dint of being mothers, to our understanding and ordering of public, political space? Instead, mothers are either being exhorted to return to their instincts and stay at home (on which more later) or to make their stand in the boardroom – to 'lean in', to use the ghastly imperative in the title of Sheryl Sandberg's bestseller – as if being the props of neo-liberalism were the most that mothers can aspire to, the highest form of social belonging and agency they can expect. We are now witnessing what feminist sociologist Angela McRobbie has described as a 'neo-liberal intensification of mothering' – perfectly turned-out, middle-class, mainly white mothers, with their perfect jobs, perfect husbands and marriages, whose permanent glow of self-satisfaction is intended to make all women who do not conform to that image (because they are poorer or black or their lives are just more humanly complicated) feel like total failures; one of McRobbie's articles on the topic has the title 'Notes on the Perfect'.[11] This has the added advantage of letting governments, whose austerity policies always disproportionately target the most vulnerable women and mothers with no chance of ever achieving such an ideal, completely off the hook.

The only good news is that the sheer amount of effort that goes into the stereotype – perhaps into all stereotypes – also bears witness to its vacuity, to the fact that it is hanging by a thread. Mothers, we might say, are the original subversives, never – as feminism has long insisted – what they seem, or are meant to be. The evidence is there, in the many brilliant chronicles I will be discussing later in this book. And yet, despite these testimonies – steadily increasing in voice and volume – the acuity and rage of mothers somehow continue to be one of the best-kept secrets of our times. I have never met a single mother (myself included) who is not far more complex, critical, at odds with the set of clichés she is meant effortlessly to embody, than she is being encouraged – or rather instructed – to think.

A very peculiar form of socially licensed aggression is at play, one that never misses its opportunity. In December 2016, calls went out in the UK to stop mothers involved in separation and child-contact cases – 70 per cent of which involve domestic violence – being routinely interrogated by abusive ex-partners in secret hearings in the civil family courts, a practice outlawed in criminal cases. One woman was forced to watch a video of her disclosing sexual abuse while sitting next to the man in question (how this had been allowed to happen was never made clear).[12] More subtly but no less insidiously, when Theresa May was elected prime minister in July 2016 after the Brexit referendum, one minister she retained – in the midst of a reshuffle generally acknowledged as intended to kill off David Cameron's legacy for ever – was the hugely unpopular Jeremy Hunt at the Department of Health, so he could complete the process of imposing his new contract on junior doctors, after massive protests and strikes. According to his department's own assessment, the contract is likely to 'impact disproportionately on women', notably mothers, due to its unsocial hours. As the Medical Women's Federation has pointed out, the most affected will be those engaged in part-time training, as well as carers and lone parents (the DH helpfully suggests that those affected should make 'informal childcare arrangements'). Lawyers have advised that the new contract might be in breach of junior doctors' right to a family life under the Human Rights Act. 'Any indirect adverse effect on women,' the DH report concluded, 'is a proportionate means of achieving a legitimate aim.'[13]

Singlehandedly and carelessly, this new contract will cut off many women's, notably mothers', access to the top ranks of the medical profession, making the job of nursing rather than consultancy or surgery their only available path – women as nurses conforming to another stereotype. One newspaper report on the dispute had the title 'The new junior doctors' contract is blatantly sexist – so why doesn't Jeremy Hunt care?'[14] Caring might be the problem – permitted on condition that it is hived off into a type of gender-specific, low-grade, women-only quarantine. As if a dedicated neo-liberal society can acknowledge the role of women as carers, but only so far, and certainly not if it disrupts any of the other arrangements by which it believes it can most efficiently perpetuate itself. All this takes place with blithe disregard for the indispensable role of mothers in securing any future whatsoever (motherhood as the downside of the modern world).

*

In July 2015, a report issued by the Equality and Human Rights Commission stated that every year in the UK a staggering 54,000 women lose their jobs as a result of their pregnancy.[15] Seventy-seven per cent of women and new mothers in work experience some form of negative treatment (bullying, snide remarks, straight insults, the suggestion that they are a burden on their employers and the state). Overall, the vast majority of pregnant women face unlawful discrimination or adverse experiences each year (77 per cent of pregnant women and new mothers face discrimination in the workplace compared with 45 per cent a decade ago).[16] Under present law, they have three months to file a case (an impossibility for most women reluctant to do so during their pregnancy).[17] The problem seems to be getting considerably worse – those estimated 54,000 women fired are double the number reported in 2005. In 2016, Citizens Advice reported a 25 per cent increase over the previous year in people seeking advice on pregnancy and maternity issues.[18] Maternity Action is demanding that the legal protection for pregnant women provided by the Maternity and Parental Leave Regulations (Regulation 10) be extended to include the period of notification of a pregnancy to six months after returning to work, the time when women are most vulnerable.

'The government's approach,' commented Maria Miller, chair of the 2016 parliamentary report on workplace discrimination, 'lacks urgency and bite' (promising a review of the situation, the report rejected the demand for a German-style ban on employers making women redundant during and after pregnancy other than in exceptional circumstances).[19] For women at the recruitment stage, there is no redress – if you are visibly pregnant at interview, you are very unlikely to get the job. Likewise, in the US, women are meant to be legally protected against discrimination, but they are not. Between 1935 and 1968, the principle was written into federal policy that women with children were unemployable.[20] The situation has barely improved. One woman, working for Procter & Gamble's Dolce & Gabbana cosmetics shop at Saks Fifth Avenue in 2014, was told, when she mentioned that one day she would like to be a mother: 'Pregnancy is not part of the uniform.' In February 2015, at four months pregnant, after needing first to sit down at moments during her shift, and then short respite periods built into her day – agreed by the management – she was fired.[21]

The law needs to be changed, but the problem goes deeper. A friend of mine with a baby under a year old was about to return to work, hoping to conceive her second child in the coming year. She fretted that this would be seen as abusing the system of legally stipulated maternity leave. The idea that everyone in her office, indeed everyone full stop, relies on women having babies – witness the instant social panic at any hint of a falling birth rate – or that she should feel free to plan her pregnancies in the way that felt right for her and her family, did not occur to her (personally, I was just impressed that she didn't seem fazed by the prospect of two babies under the age of two). Nor was she aware that, were she not in a job with such legal guarantees written into her contract, she would most likely be sacked. She felt guilty. Struggling not to allow motherhood to take over her life completely, she had nonetheless bought into the belief that it was something everyone, apart from her and her baby, should be protected from, something that should not interfere with anything or anybody else.

No less shocking – in some ways more so – nearly half (41 per cent) of all pregnant women in the UK face risks to their health and safety at work. Four per cent of pregnant women and new mothers in the workplace – a figure Maternity Action calls 'astounding' – resign from their jobs because of health and safety concerns. The existing obligation on all employers to carry out a risk assessment that considers female employees is, they state, 'woefully inadequate'.[22] Legally, if an employer refuses, or is unable, to make the working environment safe for these women then they are entitled to be suspended on full pay. It doesn't happen. Maternity Action is demanding that a 'no safe work' leave be legally formalised. Instead, women in such conditions are forced to take early maternity or sick leave, sign themselves off, as if, once again, it were their own bodies and health at fault.

As feminism has long pointed out, most bodily experiences of women from menstruation to pregnancy to menopause without distinction tend to be regarded as a form of debilitation or illness: too much blood and guts, bodies either too wet or too dry, bodies that inconveniently blur the boundaries between inside and out. Punishing pregnant women and mothers is part of a pattern (British maternity pay is among the worst in Europe, behind, for example, Croatia, Poland, Hungary, the Czech Republic, Estonia, Italy, Spain and France).[23] Although we should never underestimate the effects of an increasingly ruthless, profit-driven global economy, it seems that in all these cases there is something far more than a cost–benefit analysis involved. The same employers who provide routine assessments for workers with a health condition, an injury or disability are still refusing individual risk assessments for pregnant women and new mothers. To add insult to injury, 10 per cent of pregnant women in the UK are discouraged by their employers from attending antenatal clinics, putting their health and that of the unborn baby at risk.

So if I had been more honest with my friend, I would not just have pointed out that everyone needs mothers, or at least *some* women to be mothers, and that being a mother is hardly an antisocial activity. I would have added that, while this much is undoubtedly true, and a banal fact of life, we should never underestimate the sadism that mothers can provoke. I probably would have been somewhat apologetic (as if merely having such an ugly thought made me personally responsible for this sorry state of affairs). The reasons for this are many, as we will see, but one reason why motherhood is often so disconcerting seems to be its uneasy proximity to death. First, in the risks of childbearing, which vary so dramatically across race and class: in the US, non-Hispanic black, American Indian, Alaska Native and Puerto Rican women have the highest infant-mortality rates, the disparity between non-Hispanic blacks and whites having more than doubled over the past decade;[24] in the UK, 66 per cent of the female prison population are mothers, and twice as many black women are incarcerated than white for the same offences, while asylum seekers and refugees account for 14 per cent of all maternal deaths (despite comprising only 0.5 per cent of the population).[25] But also in the sense, less tangible but no less powerful, that the fact of being born can act as an uncanny reminder that once upon a time you were not here, and one day you will be no more. 'We have a winding sheet in our Mother's womb, which grows with us from our conception,' John Donne wrote, 'and we come into the world, wound up in that winding sheet, for we come to seek a grave.'[26] More simply, being born – each time testimony to the monumental physical and mental strength of all mothers – also alerts us to the irreducible frailty of life. Mothers require protection, solace and support from the first moment they find themselves the bearers of new life. Instead, you would think that mothers were the danger against which the workplace needs to protect itself.

The figures speak for themselves. Employers do not want pregnant women and new mothers on the premises, or if they do, they do not want them healthy and safe, nor for them to attend the clinics that will protect their well-being and the lives of their unborn babies. 'If Americans Love Moms,' the *New York Times* headlined a recent article by Nicholas Kristoff, 'Why Do We Let Them Die?'[27] He is reporting on the fact that the US mortality rate for mothers in pregnancy or childbirth is higher than in any other country in the industrialised world: 'We love mothers or at least we say we do. We are lying.'[28] The message, spoken and unspoken, is clear: we will not take care of you, or allow you to take care of yourself, because part of us wants you out of here, or dead. The visceral fact of motherhood, the *fons et origo* of our being in the world, is an affront to normal – meaning, free of mothers and babies – life. There is a crucial feminist point to be made here. The problem for everyone, but especially men, Adrienne Rich writes in her path-breaking *Of Woman Born: Motherhood as Experience and Institution* (1976), is that 'all human life on the planet is born of woman' (the first line of her book). 'There is much to suggest,' she continues, 'that the male mind has always been haunted by the force of the idea of *dependence on a woman for life itself*.'[29]

*

The subject of mothers is thick with idealisations, which have been among the foremost targets of feminist critique (ideals are one of the surest ways of punishing others as well as oneself). 'Stop peddling the myth of the perfect mother' has been the recent plaint of the founder of Net-mums, one of the biggest UK parenting websites, set up in 2000.[30] It is one of the most striking characteristics of discourse on mothering that the idealisation does not let up as the reality of the world makes the ideal harder for mothers to meet. If anything, it seems to intensify. This is not quite the same as saying that mothers are always to blame, although the two propositions are surely linked. As austerity and inequality increase across the globe, more and more children are falling into poverty, more and more families are fighting a rearguard action to protect their children from inexorable social decline. Social unrest is therefore likely to increase. In this context, as in so many moments of crisis, focus on mothers is a sure-fire diversionary tactic, not least because it so effectively deflects what might be far more disruptive forms of social critique. Mothers always fail. It will be central to my argument that such failure should not be viewed as catastrophic but as normal, that failure should be seen as part of the task. But because mothers are seen as our point of entry into the world, there is nothing easier than to make social deterioration look like something that it is the sacred duty of mothers to prevent – a type of socially upgraded version of the tendency in modern families to blame mothers for everything. This neatly makes mothers guilty, not just for the ills of the world, but also for the rage that the unavoidable disappointments of an individual life cannot help but provoke.

Hunt's new doctors' contract is by no means the first time lone mothers have been targeted for especially vindictive treatment. One of the earliest proposed measures of Tony Blair's 1997 government was to cut benefits to single mothers. This so went against the supposed humanitarian ethos of New Labour that he immediately had to back down. But his move was symptomatic of the way single mothers have often borne the brunt of a particular form of punitive social attention. In troubled times, the most vulnerable always tend to be the easiest targets of hatred. But might there also be a connection between the demand for singular devotion so regularly directed at mothers and the hostility that single mothers – who, even if not by choice, could be said to be obeying this injunction to the letter – have historically provoked? As if the single mother brings too close to the surface the utter craziness, not to say the unmanageable nature, of the idea that a mother should exist for her child and nothing else.

A single mother also stands as a glaring rebuke to the family ideal. In the US, the number of single mothers has nearly doubled over the past fifty years.[31] Throughout the 1980s and 1990s, the number of lone, including unmarried, mothers in the UK rose faster than at any other time in history, seemingly unaffected by an increasingly strident Conservative rhetoric of blame. The most pervasive image was of an unemployed teenager who had deliberately got herself pregnant to claim benefits, although as Pat Thane and Tanya Evans point out in their 2012 study of twentieth-century unmarried motherhood, she was 'very rarely to be found'.[32] Over the past century, single mothers have variously received the epithets of 'sinners, scroungers, saints' (the title of Thane and Evans's book). The first and last string them between religious opprobrium and holiness (neither of this world), the second more prosaically casts them as objects of moral contempt. Although today the religious vocabulary is somewhat muted, by depicting Bimbo Ayelabola in the unmistakeable guise of a welfare 'leech', the *Sun* headline was therefore following a tradition ('saint' is hardly an epithet about to be applied to foreigners).

Long before the migration crisis provided its image of the alien, invading mother, the single mother, it seems, was the original 'scrounger', the term that allows a cruelly unequal society to turn its back on those it has itself thrown to the bottom of the social scrapheap. This manipulative, undeserving mother was the perfect embodiment of the so-called 'dependency' culture, an idea that is being revived today in the UK in order to justify an even more full-scale dismantling of the welfare state, and more widely in the global North as part of austerity measures that target social provision above all else. 'In a country where many children do without homes and food,' Michelle Harrison writes in a report issued in Canada by the Metis Women of Manitoba, 'it is easier to punish one pregnant woman than to alleviate the condition of many.'[33]

Again, it is also worth noticing how far the real vulnerability and needs of a single mother, not to speak of those of the child or children for whom she has responsibility, seem to work in her disfavour. Lone parents, especially unmarried mothers, are still one of the poorest groups in Britain; it is estimated that they will lose 18 per cent in the universal credit squeeze.[34] According to a 2013 US census, single mothers earn an average income of $24,000 compared with the $80,000 earned by married couples with children.[35] As if genuine neediness – being, or having once been, the baby of a mother – is what Conservative rhetoric hates most. Perhaps when right-wing politicians screw up their noses at scroungers, asylum seekers and refugees, it is their own vaguely remembered years of utter dependency that they are trying, and instructing us, to repudiate. The one who most loudly promotes the ideal of ironclad self-sufficiency must surely have the echo of the baby in the nursery hovering somewhere at the back of his or her – mostly his – head.

We should also remember that it was not until 1973 in the UK that, following divorce or separation, mothers gained equal custody rights over their children. The father was legally the sole parent and a mother was only granted custody of her children until the age of seven. Up until the 1920s a woman was only free to apply to the courts for equal custodianship if she was legally married. A single woman was robbed of her children, tarred with deficiency, as if she herself were the reason for the economic constraints and social exclusion from which she was likely to suffer. In fact, the prejudice was no respecter of class. The nineteenth-century aristocrat Caroline Norton was denied all access to her three sons when she finally left her physically abusive and profligate husband (he subsequently failed to tell her when one of them suffered a fatal accident).

Historically, single mothers are not the exception. Throughout the twentieth century the number of single mothers in the UK was high, matched by the levels of illegitimacy precipitated by both the First and the Second World Wars (during the wars, with so many men at the front, single motherhood was something of a norm). The perfect family model of a married heterosexual couple, against which single mothers are so harshly measured, is an anomaly, a mere blip of the statistics, typical only between 1945 and 1970. When Pat Thane laid this out in 2010 in 'Happy Families? History and Family Policy', the question mark of the title was the giveaway and provocation. Her pamphlet provoked an outcry from Conservatives and family lobbyists determined to prove the lasting damage inflicted on children by family breakdown and the unconventional child-rearing arrangements that have been its consequence (I am inclined to think that the real scandal might have been the idea that a single mother, however hard her life, might also be happy).[36] Although absentee fathers are also indicted, the barely hidden subtext of this rhetoric is that single mothers cannot be entrusted with the care of their own children. In the UK, the number of young women who had their children forcibly removed for adoption over three decades from the 1950s to the 1970s is only today coming to light (in October 2016, the Catholic Church issued an open apology leading to calls for a public inquiry).[37] The irony is glaring. Mothers in the home are expected to manage more or less on their own – one of feminism's loudest, most persistent and fairest complaints – but the one thing a mother cannot possibly manage by herself is mothering.

It is, of course, a predominantly white, middle-class domestic ideal that is being promoted, one which fewer and fewer families can possibly live up to. But that has not prevented it from spreading down the class spectrum and across all ethnic groups, trampling over the 'mother-work' of women of colour, which, as Patricia Hill Collins, scholar of African American studies, was the first of many to insist, cuts across private and public, and is not corralled inside the family unit. Instead such work plays a crucial role in collective, community survival in a racially discriminating world, thereby unsettling just about every white-dominated dichotomy on the subject of mothers.[38] Today the relationship between white mothers and mothers of colour is repeating an age-old history, especially in the US, as undocumented migrants take care of the children of white middle-class mothers, relieving them of the burden of childcare so they can parade the seamless compatibility of their professional and domestic lives.

When Zoë Baird, nominated for attorney general in 1993, was found to be employing two undocumented Peruvian immigrants, one as a babysitter, there was a public uproar for her violation of immigration law prohibiting the hiring of illegal aliens. The practice, it turned out, was widespread, though no one, least of all the hiring mothers, wanted to talk about it. Notably absent in the outcry over the case of Baird, who had to step down as potential attorney general, was the slightest concern for the migrant mothers themselves.[39] Their working conditions are often inhuman. Maria de Jesus Ramos Hernandez left her three children in Mexico to work for a household in California, where she was repeatedly raped by her employer, who threatened her with jail as an illegal migrant if she did not submit. Her case received little attention, but the story is typical. These migrant women, who so often have to leave their own children behind, are mostly paid a pittance. Once again lost motherhood is the tale behind other forms of exploitation. Like Bimbo Ayelabola, they are accused of leeching off the welfare system (a charge previously targeted at job-stealing migrant men). In fact, they are being used as a cheap labour force that greases the economy while allowing other mothers to get rich. Solidarity among mothers, across class and ethnic boundaries, is not something Western cultures seem in any hurry to promote.

*

It is, therefore, immensely reassuring to register the instances of women organising against the forms of prejudice and social exclusion directed towards those mothers who have tried, and are still trying, against the harshest material odds, to create a viable life for themselves. In 1918, the pioneering National Council for the Unmarried Mother and her Child was set up in the UK to support such women, and is still active today (renamed the National Council for One Parent Families in 1970; since 2009 as Gingerbread, with which it merged in 2007). Its history includes moments of unlikely solidarity. During the First World War, the Prince of Wales Fund decided not to support unmarried mothers. One of their midwives told the executive committee about a 'respectable married woman' she had attended the previous day who had said she was happy to 'wash herself and leave her child unwashed' so that the midwife could go to plead the cause of unmarried mothers.[40]

A report on mother and baby hostels set up during the Second World War – another moment when unmarried mothers were the target of moral panic – describes how the matrons turned desolate premises into havens for 'utterly friendless girls' who may never before have known a home or 'whose parents set their own petty respectability above the ordinary decencies of human relationships'.[41] The girls would leave the hostels 'with a great deal more confidence than when they arrived'.[42] The report was never published.

Note, too, the sexual undertow (these girls are not 'respectable'). One of the greatest wartime fears was that single girls would become pregnant by black American servicemen, with dire consequences for the race of the nation and potentially for the servicemen themselves. 'Any English girl who walks out, however harmlessly, with a coloured American soldier,' a lady-in-waiting to Queen Mary, the Queen Mother, wrote to Violet Markham in 1942, 'should be made to understand that she will very probably cause his death.'[43] In the same breath her remark manages to express solicitude for the girl and the soldier, and raw prejudice against the idea of 'mixed marriages' and their potential offspring.

During the First World War, Markham had been secretary to an official investigation into suggested 'immorality' among servicewomen stationed in France. The charge was common. Gail Lewis, sociologist and writer on race and gender, was born to a white mother and a black father. In a conversation written as an open letter to her mother, Lewis quotes Major-General Arthur Arnold Bullick Dowler, who in 1942 wrote a secret missive, 'Notes on Relations with Coloured Troops': 'White women should not associate with coloured men. It follows then, that they should not walk out, dance, or drink with them. Do not think such action hard or unsociable. They do not expect your companionship and such relations would in the end only result in strife' (the letter was published in the first volume of *Studies in the Maternal*, one of the most open-minded online journals on the complexity of mothering). The fallout from these attitudes would track Lewis for the rest of her life. 'How others cast you', she addresses her mother, 'as sexually depraved and morally bankrupt.'[44] A white mother bearing a black child surpassed all understanding.

As so often in relation to mothers, something about sexuality – its pleasures and dangers – is at play (this too will be my refrain). It is another common assumption that a single mother is a woman who puts her sexual life ahead of her social responsibility. She therefore has only herself, or rather her voracious sexual appetites, to blame. Manipulative or sexual, the single mother exhibits either too much control over her sexual life or not enough – what is hardly ever mentioned in relation to teenage pregnancies is the possibility of child abuse and rape. Behind the idea of maternal virtue, therefore, another demand and/or reproach. A mother is a woman whose sexual being must be invisible. She must save the world from her desire – thereby allowing the world to conceal the unmanageable nature of all human sexuality, and its own voraciousness, from itself (as if sexuality never exists outside the bounds of married life).

Even in the years leading up to the 1960s, when there was more sympathy for the predicament of single mothers, the basic assumption was there. 'Innocent' girls could get into trouble and merited understanding provided, in the words of Thane and Evans in the opening pages of their book, 'they did not flaunt their transgressions.'[45] Nor is the childless woman immune from sexual taint. 'Surely,' as one journalist summed up a common presumption about the declining birth rate in twenty-first century France, 'a woman who refuses to be a mother enjoys lovemaking rather too much?'[46] The shudder of disapproval barely conceals its own excitement. At whatever point of the spectrum – no babies or illegitimate babies or too many babies – women find themselves caught in a steel vice (the most recent version being the charge that excessively reproducing mothers are responsible for climate change).[47]

I started this chapter by asking: what are mothers being asked to carry, what forms of failure and injustice are they made accountable for, above all, in the modern Western world? What are the fears we lay on mothers, both as accusation and demand (the one following the other)? Why do we expect mothers to subdue the very fears we ourselves have laid at their door? For much of the rest of this book, in dialogue with some of the most searching writing on mothers, I will be attempting some kind of answer. In the meantime, since the most powerful ideologies of motherhood present themselves as eternal and unchanging – from here to maternity – the question must be: has it always been thus? After all, it is one of the first principles of feminism that, if you want to challenge a stereotype, especially one masquerading as nature or virtue or essence, if your aim is to drag it down from its pedestal or yank it up from the dirt where it festers, then try and find where it all started. Better still, look to a place and time when – maybe – it was not even there.

THEN

There was a time when becoming a mother meant no loss of a woman's role in vital forms of public life. In Ancient Greece, a woman was maiden, bride and then, after childbirth, mature female. This was hardly a life of freedom. Young girls of thirteen and fourteen were married off to men in their thirties. Women, like slaves, were not citizens (the woman/slave analogy eloquent in itself). A woman could fulfil her destiny only as a mother. But according to one account of Greek motherhood, in doing so she did not cease to be involved in civic space, notably in the community of women who participated in religious ceremonies.[1] It was the single arena in which women enjoyed parity or even superiority vis-à-vis men. Women held priestly office and performed ceremonial duties, such as at the Eleusinian Mysteries in honour of the goddess Demeter and at the Panathenian festivals that celebrated the Athenian patron goddess Athena (they appear everywhere in the Ionic frieze of the Parthenon, the most important religious building in the city).[2] Women played an important role in the cult activity that fostered the welfare of the household (*oikos*) and city, including the ritual commemoration of the dead.[3] Such activity enabled them to intervene in the politics of their community, granting them, in the words of classics scholar Barbara Goff, 'significant presence and agency in the public realm' (as she also points out, ritual itself was a type of work).[4] Although ancient Athens was undoubtedly a patriarchal society, scholars have argued that names, property and priesthoods could all travel through the female line.[5]

Visits to temples both before and after the birth of a child gave the mother considerable access to the community beyond the domestic boundaries of the home.[6] On becoming a mother, the woman therefore maintained her ties to a realm that exceeded the domain of motherhood itself, an idea that modern times seem progressively to have lost. 'Parenthood is not a transition,' Rachel Cusk writes in *A Life's Work: On Becoming a Mother* (2001), 'but a defection, a political act.'[7] After the birth of her first child, Cusk felt she had been left stranded on the far shore of any viable political life. Her horizons narrowed. She was cut down to size. Cusk is pointing out that this isolation from the wider world – separate spheres, as it was first defined in the nineteenth century – is as sudden as it is absolute (this regardless of whether today's mother eventually returns to work). But it is neither natural nor eternal. It is a piece of history, and should be recognised both as personally damaging and as a fully political fact.

A few years earlier, in 1998, Melissa Benn wrote of the way modern mothers seem 'encased in a new silence . . . We know what we do, but we don't talk about it publicly.'[8] She praised the new-found forms of community and solidarity she encountered among mothers while researching her book, but she also noted the restricted compass of mothers talking mainly, sometimes only, to each other. In fact, in the UK and the US, a mother's separation from the polity has by no means always been the norm. There is a long tradition going back to the eighteenth century of seeing motherhood as part of civic life. The role of the mother was to generate the new citizen, and the nation's stability was seen to reside in the civic virtue she cultivated in her child – although, since the mother was confined to the home, this only granted her, in historian Linda Colley's words, a 'public role of a kind'.[9]

In 451–450 BC, Pericles, orator, statesman and a general of Athens, passed a law that made citizenship conditional on descent from an Athenian mother as well as a father, excluding all *xenos*, or foreign 'outsiders'.[10] The Athenian mother therefore played a key role in transmitting the citizenship from which she herself was debarred (that she was being used to block the civic status of alien mothers has a chilling resonance in today's anti-migrant world). Scholars are divided as to whether this increased or lowered her status, as they are as to whether the virtue of the mother's femininity in relation to husband and child was freighted with the duty of securing the viability of nation and city space.

Either way, as classics scholar Edith Hall has pointed out, the frequency with which Greek men enunciated their ideal of femininity suggests that women by no means always conformed to it.[11] Athenian women uttering obscenities and handling pastry models of genitalia during the winter Haloa festival at Eleusis may have acted as a safety valve, but such practices also indicate that the dominant codes aimed at securing the role of successful wife and mother for women were, as Goff puts it, 'always at risk'.[12] According to Thucydides, women joined in the fourth-century revolution in Kerkyra (Corfu), throwing tiles onto the heads of the oligarchs from the roofs (this also appears to have been viewed as an acceptable activity for women in times of siege).[13] Speeches from the ancient courts of law show women, despite the severest restrictions on their legal rights, determined to do all they could to maximise their influence.[14]

Attic drama suggests this independent spirit was nowhere more present than in relation to mothers, who are portrayed as citizens, chorus, subjects on the world's stage. This can help us – it certainly has helped me – to envisage alternative ways of thinking about the real and imagined political selfhood of being a mother. At moments, Greece and Rome – with Shakespeare in a walk-on part – will appear as inspirational, at others as scarily familiar. Not for nothing is Greece, in the famously Eurocentric formula, referred to as 'cradle' or 'birthplace' of the West – or 'the mother of us all', as one might say. We should be wary, of course – classical culture is not the only way of tracking the path from now to then. But, as scholars from Mary Beard to Edith Hall have convincingly argued, the Greeks are still with us today, even as Beard issues the salutary caution that our grip on classical times is fragile. As ancient historian Esther Eidinow writes, the sparse evidence throws 'only the faintest of silhouettes down through time', even while her study of witch trials in fourth-century Athens is aimed at retrieving the agency and power of these women.[15]

There are, however, few testimonies available from the mothers of Ancient Greece themselves, who, in the words of Lauren Hackworth Petersen and Patricia Salzman-Mitchell, editors of a volume on the topic, 'left little trace of their own existence' (a lot of examples are taken by necessity from funeral urns).[16] Hence my focus on drama, which has survived more or less intact and where different versions of motherhood, for better or worse, could be tried out for size, admittedly written by men. My engagement with classical culture on the subject of mothers has left me alternately cheering and tearing my hair (although, as we will see, by the time I have finished the two responses start to coalesce).

In Euripides' *The Suppliant Women*, Aethra pleads with her son Theseus to be allowed to speak on behalf of the Argive mothers whose fallen sons lie unburied. The play can be read as a mother-centred version of the better-known *Antigone*, whose more famous heroine insists on her brother's sacred right to due burial against unjust man-made law. In *The Suppliant Women*, Aethra makes her plea, not for a brother against the state, but in the name of the city and on behalf of mothers who are not her kin. When Theseus first objects that these grieving women of Argos are foreigners, she replies: 'You do not belong to them. Shall I say something, my son, that brings honour to you and the city?'[17] Defying him in the name of a cross-national community of mothers, she presents her case in terms of the contribution women make to the civic good: if he ignores their plea, the city over which he rules will be destroyed.

Aethra is drawing on the authority owing to her as mother of the Athenian king. Theseus concedes, and then proceeds to a passionate defence of democracy: 'This city is free, and ruled by no one man. The people reign in annual alterations. / And they do not yield their power to the rich; / the poor man has an equal share in it.'[18] As if to say: in relation to democracy, listening to the voice of bereaved, disenfranchised mothers is the true litmus test. The modern world could helpfully take note. In November 2016, the Mothers of the Movement, bereaved mothers of some of the highest-profile black victims of police violence in the US, started travelling the country to tell the stories of their dead children and to speak out on police racism, gun violence and criminal justice reform. 'I had to change my mourning into a movement, my pain into purpose and sorrow into a strategy,' states Gwen Carr, mother of Eric Garner, killed on Staten Island, New York, in 2014, aged forty-three. 'I know it's too late for Eric but we have to save the unborn.' 'When it's time to speak, I go forth. I'm not a politics person. I mean, I guess I am now, in some ways' – the words of Valerie Bell, mother of Sean Bell, shot in Queens, New York, in 2006, aged twenty-three.[19] Another modern instance of mothers forging a political voice out of tragedy.

In *The Suppliant Women*, Theseus himself ends up joining the grieving mothers as they wash the wounded corpses of their dead, vanquished sons. He enters the role of a mother, becomes one of their kind. When Adrastus, king of defeated Argos, hears of this he expresses dismay: 'That was a dreadful burden, bringing shame,' the messenger replies. 'How can humanity's common ills be shameful?'[20] Victorious kings rarely embrace the bodies of the defeated (any more than do policemen with guns on the street). Theseus' act is all the more extraordinary in a democracy where political freedom in the city space was seen to rely on keeping the crude necessities of life behind closed doors, which also meant that the paterfamilias, the kyrios or *dominus*, ruled over his family and slaves with a rod of iron.[21]

Today, of course, in most countries in the world,

women are citizens. Mothers can be leaders and fully enter the *polis*, although it's worth noting that neither Angela Merkel nor Theresa May have children. In the case of May, when Andrea Leadsom, one of her rivals for the role of prime minister after the Brexit referendum of June 2016, suggested that this fact rendered her unfit for office, she had to withdraw from the leadership election.

It is, however, still the case that today, in public, the bodily necessities of mothering are brushed under the carpet and/or consigned to another hidden, intimate world. Perhaps the dismay provoked by Theseus' compassionate gesture allows us to speculate why. It is not just so that men can keep their hands clean – to which some men would fairly reply that today they share the housework and change nappies (we have moved on from 1972 when *New Society* reported that it was a rare father who could change his child's nappy).[22] Rather, the problem goes the other way. The radical care and visceral mess of child-rearing must neither degrade nor stain the upstanding citizen. The shameful debris of the human body, familiar to any mother, must not enter the domain of public life and spill onto the streets. I remember once trying to persuade a young university colleague that she shouldn't hesitate to bring her baby to work as the need arose, first simply as a practical matter so she could get to work and make her life liveable, but perhaps, even more, so that the stuff that mothers deal with on a daily basis should be *seen*.

Always I am on the lookout for those moments when mothers get to speak the unspeakable, trash the expectations laid upon them, play with other ideas. If the main function of a married woman in Ancient Greece and Rome was to provide fodder for the war machine, for many women this was not a tempting prospect (one effective herbal abortifacient made available to women was so popular it became extinct, the herb featuring on Cyrene coinage alongside the figure of a woman).[23] At a key moment in *The Suppliant Women*, Adrastus laments the defeat of his nation. When the chorus, made up of the grieving mothers and their handmaidens, pleads, 'No word for the mothers?' he replies: 'O wretched mothers of children! / Behold a sea of troubles.'[24] This is tragic, but also hand-wringing and lyrical to the point of banality. Once again, pathos neutralises a far more radical complaint. The chorus is swift in its judgement: 'Would that my body had never been yoked to a husband's bed.'[25]

What is the point of breeding sons with the sole aim of sending them to battle? In Sparta, girls benefited from being married off later than in other Greek states, but only because the Spartans realised that they were more likely to produce a healthy warrior child.[26] The suppliant women are in revolt (not so suppliant after all). They turn against their destiny – and their husbands – because they can see the reality of the cruel political world they are being asked to gestate. Perhaps that is another reason why mothers are unwelcome in public spaces, integrated with difficulty into the political scene. If they really entered the world without let or inhibition, they would read it; they would see and lay bare its intolerable cruelty for what it truly is (speaking truth to power). In Britain, after the First World War, women turned their pain to political ends, demanding the vote as the fair if partial recompense for having been expected to send their sons to war.[27]

But there must always be the risk that the mothers of soldiers just might decide that a world at war is worthy neither of their labour nor of the dedicated, albeit unchosen, futures of their offspring. In Euripides' *Medea*, well before the heroine kills her two sons, the act for which she and the play are infamous, the chorus announces in one of its longest speeches that they have pondered and concluded that those who do not have children are happier by far: no shadow of care, no unknowing as to whether your labours will produce good or bad children, no endless dread that, in the worst and final disaster, Death may take your child.[28] This is the bleakest view, half the story, or not even half the story, some mothers would say. But, as feminism has long pointed out, by refusing to be mothers, women have the power to bring the world to its end.

*

In Ancient Greece, the line between fighting and child-birth went deep, as the dangers of childbearing were spliced into the fields of war. This blurs the inviolable distinction between life and death that we expect mothers, of all people, to keep intact. It also stalls in its tracks any possible sentimentality on the subject of mothers, a sentimentality with which the modern world, in denial of its own violence, is still saturated. These lines spoken by Medea early in the play are among the most well known, often lifted clean out from under her murder of her own children as a stand-alone feminist plaint:

> They, men, allege that we enjoy a life
> secure from danger safe at home,
> while they confront the thrusting spears of war.
> I would rather join
> the battle rank of shields three times
> than undergo birth's labour once.

Her list of grievances is long: women are obliged to accept a husband as 'master of our body', to keep 'our eye on him alone', whereas the man is free; women are the most beset by trials of 'any species that has breath of power and thought'.[29]

Medea is not alone in making her analogy between parturition and the injuries of war. According to Plutarch, a Greek living under the Roman Empire, the only exceptions to the rule against naming the dead on their tombstones were men who fell in battle and women who died in childbirth: the woman, producer of the future citizens of the city state, bore childbirth 'just as the warrior bears the enemy's assault, by struggling against pain: giving birth is a battle.' 'Not just a symmetry,' the feminist classics scholar Nicole Loraux writes in her 1981 article, 'Le Lit, la guerre' ('In bed, at war'), 'it is more like an act of exchange or at the very least the presence of war at the heart of childbirth.' Likewise, men become women, as the pain of a wounded soldier is compared to labour: 'Fortune and misfortune of the warrior: to break all limits, including that of the virility he ostensibly embodies, in order to suffer like a woman.'[30] In a wondrously gender-confounding moment, war blurs the distinction of the sexes in relation to the very acts – battle, childbirth – normally seen as their most representative and distinctive of roles. It reduces dying men to the state of women as the bearers of new life, while also giving only to both of them the right to be named for posterity on their tombs. Who then, soldiers or birthing mothers, are the true heroes? The answer must surely be neither or both. In which case, perhaps, Loraux suggests, we should not be in too much of a hurry to charge Greek thought with misogyny.

By the time of Shakespeare's Roman plays, this analogy will receive one of its most violent, exultant affirmations in the character of Volumnia, mother of Coriolanus, who, again in a speech that has become famous, turns the link between war and maternal nurture inside out. She, too, is dismissed as close on crazy, or more charitably as exerting undue influence on her son (an example of Shakespeare's 'suffocating' mothers).[31] In fact, she is one in a line of many mothers, as she draws on an ancient tradition to which she gives her own unique twist:

> The breasts of Hecuba
> When she did suckle Hector, look'd not lovelier
> Than Hector's forehead when it spit forth blood
> At Grecian sword contemning.[32]

These words are meant to shock or even repulse, but Volumnia is speaking the hidden truth of what a militaristic culture asks of the bodies of its mothers. For Medea, battle was preferable to the agonies of childbirth (a comparison that in the end works to the advantage of neither). For Volumnia, the blood of battle and the breasts of the nursing mother compete to win the aesthetic prize. It is not pain but beauty that violently aligns the archetypal trope of mothering – the milk of human kindness – and the spillage of war.

Volumnia is a Roman mother. Even more than in Greece, the Roman mother was monumentalised on behalf of her citizen sons. Imperial mothers like Octavia and Livia were celebrated by buildings in whose construction they also sometimes played a role: Octavia completed the renovation of the Republican portico that bore her name; Livia left an extensive portfolio of public works that rivalled that of many imperial men; women of the Julio–Claudian family under Augustus involved themselves in his programmatic rebuilding of Rome. Today's queens and wives of presidents have their realm restricted to interior design, while leading women architects are rare – Zaha Hadid, who did not have children, would be one striking exception, stating in interviews that her work would have made it impossible.[33]

But it is as the mothers of warriors that the Roman woman reaches her apogee. Shakespeare goes out of his way to make Volumnia more militaristic than his source, Plutarch, where there is less emphasis on valiancy and glory, more on the misery Coriolanus has brought upon the 'common weal'.[34] His Volumnia out-soldiers them all. 'If my son were my husband,' she insists to the perplexed and downcast Virgilia, wife of Coriolanus, who is grieving his absence in war, 'I should freer rejoice in that absence wherein he won honour, than in the embracements of his bed, where he would show most love.'[35] When he was a young man, Volumnia delighted in sending her son into battle, from which he returned victorious, his brows crowned with an oak coronet: 'Had I a dozen sons, each in my love alike, and none less dear than thine and my good Martius, I had rather eleven die nobly for their country, than one voluptuously surfeit out of action.'[36]

But, by the end of the play, Volumnia is pleading with her son, who, expelled from Rome, has formed a deadly alliance with the Volscian enemy, not to tear 'his country's bowels out' by laying waste to his natal city.[37] She finally uses her persuasive power as mother to wrest back the violence that she herself had celebrated, casting its gory shadow, unflinchingly and with such relish, across her own maternal role. But it is her own brutal eloquence, her mental immersion as a mother into the carnage of war, that has uniquely qualified her to do so.

We can pathologise Volumnia, as indeed Medea, but that is too easy. They have both tapped into a way of thinking, lost to our time, that does not require motherhood to purify and blind itself to the world's violence, or to our own: 'We know too much,' writes Adrienne Rich, 'at first hand [of] the violence which over centuries we have been told is the way of the world, but which we exist to mitigate and assuage.' 'We know too much' – Rich is implicating herself as mother in the worst of the modern world. In *Of Woman Born* (the 1995 reprint), she defends her decision to keep the final chapter on mothers and violence, which she was pressured to remove. It was read by some mothers as a betrayal (as if mothers can only be defended as humans if they are good).[38] On the other side of idealisation, war and childbirth are recognised in classical thought as two moments when the fabric of the social order is rent. Unlike today when, against all the bloody evidence, armies and mothers

– lynchpins of the social order, although at opposite poles of the human spectrum – are called upon to secure our futures and make a precarious, dangerous world feel safe.

*

We know that the male colonisation of mothers' bodies starts inside the womb. One of Donald Trump's first executive orders reinstated the 'global gag' rule that bans funding for groups anywhere in the world offering abortion or abortion advocacy, even if they use their own funds to do, which has been described as a 'death warrant for thousands of women' (one of the most notorious photos of his first one hundred days in office is of a bunch of indistinguishable men signing the order into law).[39] As well as putting the health and lives of women seeking abortion at risk, the rule will cut funding worth billions to the developing world and threatens free speech. Republican presidents regularly reinstate this rule, which had been overturned by Obama, but reproductive groups described it this time as the most extreme of its kind.[40] As I write, the *Roe v. Wade* ruling is considered to be at serious risk of being overturned for the first time since it was passed by the US Supreme Court in 1973: Neil Gorsuch, Trump's first appointment to the Supreme Court, is famous for the vehemence of his anti-abortion convictions.

But the issue of abortion is not the only form that such

colonisation can take. In 1999, the case of *Dobson* (Litigation Guardian of) *v. Dobson* was brought to the Supreme Court of Canada. A woman, whose son was born with serious impairment after a car accident in which she was deemed negligent, was sued by the maternal grandfather on behalf of her child. In the end, the charge of negligence was set aside and the decision focused entirely on whether the son, Ryan Dobson, 'has the legal capacity to bring a tort action against his mother for her allegedly negligent act which occurred while he was in utero'. Can a child sue his own mother for what she did, or failed to do, before he was born?

This, we could say, is the social punishment of mothers with a vengeance, a nightmare version of where we started, as the law extends its cold, hard reach deep inside the body of the pregnant woman, judging her culpable before life even begins. But in a judgement heralded by feminist legal scholar Diana Ginn, the judges decided for the mother on the grounds of her privacy, autonomy and the rights of women. Had they imposed a legal duty of care upon a pregnant woman towards her foetus or unborn child, the potential for curtailing women's choices and behaviour would, they acknowledged, have been 'staggering', with no 'rational' or 'principled' limit to the type of claims that might be brought (they were citing a 1993 Royal Commission on new reproductive technologies).[41] Although there was a dissenting opinion, Ginn fairly sees the result of this landmark case as striking a feminist blow for mothers, which she traces to the atmosphere fostered by Adrienne Rich's book (Ginn's essay appears in a collection celebrating *Of Woman Born* and its legacy).[42]

In a way that is again reminiscent of Greek thought, today's legal writing tends to see a pregnant woman and her foetus either as an organic unit or as a potential field of battle.[43] In the Dobson case, Judge Cory referred to the 'inseparable unit between the woman and her foetus' as the basis for taking the mother's side. Dissenting Judge Major, on the other hand, insisted that the interests of the foetus and the mother were not, and should not be, considered as one: 'It is no answer to the plaintiff in this case that unilateral concerns about a pregnant woman's competing rights are sufficient to "negative" a negligent violation of his physical integrity. His rights, too, are at stake.'[44] The distinction is legally significant but also partly illusory. Either way, the mother is being pressed to recognise, as if she did not already know, that her unborn child depends on her for life itself. Note how this obvious truth erases any concern for her social condition. Class, housing, level of nutrition, the presence or absence and behaviour of the father or partner are all wiped out of the picture. She has been placed in a social vacuum, severed, even before her baby is born, from the mundane, basic realities and pressures of a lived life.

How far, then, have we come? In relation to the bodies of mothers, we have come far, but only so far. In

Greek embryology, pregnancy is shadowed by a not wholly dissimilar idea of foetal harm. The foetus is always in potential danger from its mother, who is solely to blame if anything goes wrong, such as the birth of a premature or sickly child. *Diseases of Women*, the Hippocratic medical treatise of the fifth century BC, lists the activities that endanger the embryo, notably when the woman is sick or weak: lifting weights, jumping about, fainting, eating too much or too little, being flatulent, having a womb that is too large or too small, becoming fearful or alarmed or receiving a blow. The list is of course deranged, veering from common sense (the first two, although neither likely if she is sick or weak), to matters over which she has no control (the size of her womb), to realities – fainting, fear or alarm, receiving a blow – for which she can hardly be held responsible.

Above all, in Greek embryology, in a trope at least partly reiterated by Judge Major, the womb was a site of struggle. The victorious foetus, now too large and hungry to be fed by the mother, had to fight its way out of the maternal body, tearing the maternal membranes, thrashing about with its arms and feet. Unlike chickens, whose mothers could be relied upon to hatch their brood at the appropriate time, the human mother had to be vanquished for life to begin. Likewise in Shakespeare's time, it was believed that the pregnant mother could suffocate her foetus. In his 1635 treatise *The Nursing of Children*, Jacques Guillimeau suggests that the mother can choose to intercept her baby by strangling it in the womb. Excess feeding and 'surfetting' would have the same effect. Birth came about through the mother's deficiency, when the supply of air or food failed.[45] Guillimeau was just one of several commentators who believed that breast milk was 'whitened blood', a derivative of menstrual blood and potentially lethal.[46]

We have watched the link between childbirth and war receiving its starkest delineation in the bitter words of Greek and Roman mothers on the stage. Now we can perhaps appreciate these mothers as lifting into the public domain, seizing to their own ends – 'defamiliarising' would be Brecht's term for such radical political gestures – this image of the womb as a battleground. Tracking violence to inside their bodies, classical medical discourse made women accountable for everything that could possibly go wrong (since this is the primordial battle from which all other battles follow, that presumably also includes war itself). In one version of gestation, where the mother, as well as the father, was at least recognised as contributing to the creation of an embryo, her seed was the weakling and, in a lethal struggle, the paternal seed had to be victorious to secure the birth of a son. In the very role by which she was defined, the best thing a mother could therefore do for her unborn infant was to defeat herself.

Most disturbingly, one embryological account, without mitigation of overbearing maternal accountability

and guilt, sees the woman as playing no role in gestation. She is merely the passive recipient of the male seed
– ancillary and culpable, both. This is Apollo in *The
Eumenides*, the final play of Aeschylus' *Oresteia*, giving one of the most renowned defences of this crooked
vision:

> The woman who is called *the 'mother' of the
>   child is not the parent*,
> but rather a nurse of the newly sown embryo.
> He who impregnates generates, while *she, as a
>   stranger for a stranger*,
> preserves the shoot if the god does not harm it
>   in some way.[47]

'Stranger for a stranger' – remember that just seven
years later, in 451/450 BC, Athens will secure the citizenship of its people against all foreigners to the city. Being
a stranger to your own child therefore symbolically
wipes out any civic, political allegiance between mother
and child. Apollo presents this argument in defence of
Orestes, on trial at the court of Athena for having murdered his mother Clytemnestra in revenge for her killing
his father Agamemnon. Clytemnestra had likewise been
motivated by revenge. Agamemnon had sacrificed their
daughter Iphigenia to the gods in exchange for a fair
wind that would allow his fleet to set sail and defeat
Troy after the abduction of Helen.

Apollo's task is to explain why the murder of Agamemnon, king and husband, is more punishable than the crime of matricide. He is struggling. This is his fourth attempt – first he argues that Orestes acted on Zeus' command, then that Agamemnon, killed by treachery, was a man and a king (as if there were no treachery in matricide), then that the life of a murdered man is irrevocably lost (as if that were not true of all deaths, which must include the deaths of women). For psychoanalysis, this would be defined as the 'kettle logic' of the unconscious, a self-defeating pile-up of arguments in which each one finally wipes out the next. The chorus, on the other hand, is having none of it. In the final play of the trilogy, they are the voice of the Eumenides, or Furies, whose role is to 'hound matricides to exile'.[48] For them, Clytemnestra's crime is the less heinous because she was not of Agamemnon's blood. When Orestes retorts, 'But am I of my mother's?' they reply: 'Vile wretch! Did she not nourish you in her own womb? / Do you disown your mother's blood, which is your own?'[49]

In similar vein, in Sophocles' *Electra*, Clytemnestra claims to her enraged daughter that Agamemnon had no right to sacrifice Iphigenia when he 'did not labour an equal amount of suffering (*lypès*)'. The mother's part in childbearing is greater, with 'the quantity of pain the measure': 'he who sowed her, like the one who bore her, me'.[50] Clytemnestra will be murdered by Orestes, but she is at least given the chance to make her own case, even if doomed, before she dies. In this, ironically, she has Athenian law on her side. Marriage between half-siblings was only classified as incest if they shared the same mother (whereas marriage between half-siblings who shared a father was fine). The mother–child bond was therefore the most intimate. Apollo is making his stand against commonly felt, legally recognised belief.[51]

In Robert Icke's brilliant 2015 *Oresteia* adaptation, Clytemnestra's voice moves front of stage. Why, she asks, 'does the murder of the mother count for less than that of the father? . . . Why is the mother's motive for murder *lesser* than the son's?' She herself then provides the answer to her own question as only a woman can: 'Because the *woman* is less important.' In the London production, Lia Williams pronounced these words with biting, spaced emphasis, as if her forfeit life relied on the audience paying heed (having her testify after death on her own behalf in the courtroom is, of course, Icke's radical invention).[52] Clytemnestra is a grieving mother, bereft of a daughter whose murder by her father is the key precipitating factor, too easily erased from sight but to which Icke gives due status. 'This whole thing,' she addresses the ghost of her daughter, 'this whole thing is about *you*.' Inside the bloodied bathrobe of his dead father, Orestes finds a note stating 'Child Killer', which is projected in capitals onto a vast screen at the back of the stage.[53]

In this version, Apollo is not present at the trial. The

judgement still falls against Clytemnestra. But the doctor who speaks the truth to Orestes throughout the play states unequivocally that matricide is the greater inhuman offence: 'her act was not like yours. / Agamemnon did not lift her from her crib. / He did not breastfeed her.'[54] In Aeschylus' version, as she pleads with Orestes for her life, Clytemnestra exposes her breast, which gives him pause, but finally to no avail.

Apollo's speech in Aeschylus' text at least has the virtue of showing how the idea that mothers have no role in the creation of life leads directly to a justification for killing them. Likewise, Athena pronounces her judgement in favour of Orestes on the grounds that no mother gave her birth. In fact, this is another matricide, as her mother, the goddess Metis, is wiped out in the myth that she sprang ready formed from the head of Zeus (who had swallowed her).[55] Right at the start of the trilogy, Agamemnon tells of a portent in which two kings of birds ravenously tear the body of a pregnant hare: 'Big with her burden, now a living prey / In the last darkness of their unborn day.'[56] Aeschylus' trilogy ends with Orestes pardoned, his name restored to the royal house over the body of his dead mother. The modern version ends instead with Orestes, in a state of dizzy anxiety, repeating four times: 'What do I do?' In Colm Tóibín's retelling, *House of Names* (2017), Orestes is haunted by the cries of Clytemnestra and Iphigenia as she is being slaughtered (the mother's agony finally more important than the crime for which he kills her).[57]

'How,' asks French psychoanalyst André Green, 'is he to acquire his rightful belonging and add his name to his father's lineage, yet also destroy the means by which he came into his life?'[58] This is hatred of mothers raised to the nth degree, the bedrock, even in the teeth of progress, of what mothers are still up against. In 2015, Icke's *Oresteia* played to packed houses in London. Something in this play, even rerendered for our times, still resonates. Why, if not that mothers remain our favourite sacrificial objects, as disposable as they are indispensable to life? Why, if not that mothers continue to be the container for all our plaints, and to bear the brunt of an unjust world?

*

At some time in the 1980s, a French feminist told me that her partner had announced out of the blue that for the first time in his life he could envisage a woman as both mother and lover. I think this was meant to be the highest compliment, the implication being that, in the normal run of things, once a woman has a child she ceases to be desirable. But, he was generously reassuring her, this would not happen in her case. I don't think the mother's way of seeing things had even crossed his mind, the possibility that many mothers, out of sheer exhaustion and discomfort, not to speak of their absorption in and the demands of their baby, might, at least for a while after childbirth, lose interest in sex. Some years later, when I had just become a mother, a close friend pronounced as a kind of dire warning that any woman taking a lover while she was still the mother of a baby or young child would summon the wrath of the gods on her head. As if motherhood brings the idea of a woman as a subject of sexual desire to a complete standstill. Mothering would then be one of the ways a culture purifies itself of the sexuality that mostly still brings motherhood about today. Even if, as critic Rachel Bowlby has pointed out, the advances of reproductive technology mean we are approaching a time when we will no longer be able to assume that children come 'from two parents, of two sexes, who once had sex'.[59] Or, in the words of Elena Ferrante – to whom we will be returning – 'no one, starting with the mother's dressmaker, must think that a mother has a woman's body' (she is citing Elsa Morante, her favourite contemporary woman writer).[60]

This, too, is an old story. When Hamlet confronts his mother in the closet scene, he begins by lambasting her with the outrage of his uncle having murdered and ousted his father, but by the end of the scene, it seems that this is by no means the only, or even the main, offence: 'Who'll chide hot blood within a virgin's heart / When lust shall dwell within a matron's breast?'[61] Matron means married woman or grandmother, but the key is, of course, that she is his mother: 'You are the Queen, your husband's brother's wife, but would you were not so. You are my mother.'[62] If a mother persists as a sexual being, then the virtue of virgins – the next generation of mothers – will be destroyed. Do not, he issues his final instructions, 'let the blunt King tempt you again to bed'.[63] In Icke's *Oresteia*, the autopsy of Clytemnestra reveals that, in addition to neck and torso, her body shows stab wounds in the genitals.[64] It is not only for the killing of his father that she is being punished by her son.

But it is the mother's sensuality towards her own children that is the greatest taboo. When Victoria Beckham posted a photo on Instagram of her kissing her five-year-old daughter on the lips on her birthday in the summer of 2016, there was a public outcry (some trolls called them 'pervy' and 'lesbians'). In this, the scandals of child abuse have played their part. But, even where there is no question of abuse, the eros of the mother–child relationship, of which mothers speak to one another under their breath, still tends to be frowned upon or rarely talked about. On this matter, Ancient Greece and Rome can be seen as rather more progressive. Cleopatra, deemed the most desirable of women, was the mother of four children, one, she claimed, by Julius Caesar and the three youngest by Mark Antony, something which most representations of Cleopatra conspire to forget (although there is an allusion to her children at the end of Shakespeare's play, it tends to be overlooked, and no one I mentioned it to had the faintest idea she was a mother). In fact, the silence began with Octavian in a bid to stop his conflict with Mark Antony being seen as a civil war, his offspring potentially in arms against hers in a battle for the keys of the city state.

And Venus was referred to as *mater amoris* or 'mother of love' (how can you mother eros other than incestuously, which might be the whole point?). This is Venus in Virgil's *Aeneid* just after she has responded dismissively to her son Aeneas' charge of neglect: 'She spoke, and as she turned away, her rosy neck gleamed, while from her head her heavenly hair breathed a divine fragrance, her robes slipped down to her feet and in her step she was revealed as a true goddess.'[65] The moment is both breathless and brutal: her sexuality, her body, is exposed as the naked truth of her cruelty towards her son, who interestingly only fully recognises her as his mother at this revealing instant. But other images are less damning. The Terra Mater, a panel of the *Ara Pacis* dated 13–9 BC, shows the mother goddess and her two children with her garment slipping gently from her shoulders (as this is a sculpture the exposure stops there). She is therefore also Venus, and her sensuality is part of her tenderness towards the two boys cavorting on her lap.

The eros of mothers can be turned against them at a stroke. In one striking classical example, Lysias composes the speech for Euphiletus, who is defending himself in court against the charge of murdering the Greek citizen Eratosthenes, who was his wife's lover. To establish the harmony of their household, how intimate a place it had been before the affair, he begins by focusing on the love with which she suckled her son, before turning the tables completely by arguing that her motherly devotion was a distraction, a sensuous decoy, a plot. So dedicated did she seem that he could never have foreseen her treason. This scheming mother had even used the cries of the infant to hide her liaison. The innocence of breastfeeding slips effortlessly into guilt (as we will see in the next chapter, none of this has gone away).[66]

*

We are not done with the Greeks, although that 'we' will be qualified in what follows, because the Greek heritage is not the whole picture, or indeed ancestry, of modern times, which also has more than one story to tell. In one account, Greece in itself is indebted to an African inheritance, which the West has gone to great lengths to suppress.[67] And, in its precolonial days, Africa offers models of mothers as fully engaged social and political beings. For example, in parts of what is now known as Uganda, queen mothers controlled the alliances of the clan, though such status was quashed in the nineteenth century when they were effectively enslaved by a new alliance of native elite and British colonial men.[68] But if the Greeks are still present in our midst, there is no reason why, at moments, we should not learn from them and, at others, as we have seen in relation to Clytemnestra's tragic tale, turn to face them and issue our reply. The lines from then to now are complex, covered neither by complacency at our progress, nor nostalgia for a better age (two limited options that imitate the way we are so often encouraged to think of our relationship to mothers).

To end, then, by returning to Medea, the most irredeemable mother of them all. 'If Freud had been less preoccupied with Oedipus and more observant of Medea when he remarked that "aggression forms the basis of every relation of affection and love among people",' Nicole Loraux writes in *Mothers in Mourning*, 'he would certainly not have added: "with the single exception, perhaps, of the mother's relation to her male child."'[69] The great theorist of Oedipus, she elaborates, was blind to this strand of Greek tragic thinking, where wrath against the spouse triumphs over love for her two sons. But even this reading of *Medea* is uncertain. In other versions of the tale, in circulation before Euripides, Medea does not murder her children: hatred of Medea drives the Corinthians to kill them, or else the relatives of Creon kill them in revenge after she has murdered Creon and fled to Athens, or she puts her children through a rite designed to make them immortal, during the course of which they die.[70]

Even in Euripides' drama, what drives Medea to kill is not, or not only, her sexual rage against their father but equally the loss of his love for their children, which condemns them to an uncertain future. Her cry is for justice and that diatribe on the pains of mothering the lament of a mother whose greatest fear is that she and her children will be homeless and stateless, a condition we can surely not gloss over today (hence her plea to Creon for a stay of execution against being expelled from the city). Only in their final confrontation after the murder, when Jason accuses her of being 'stung by thoughts of sex' – 'And you believe it justified / to kill them for the sake of sex?' – does she return: 'Do you suppose such troubles to be trivial for a woman?'[71]

For the most part, it is not sex that Medea has on her mind but survival. Although she is finally given all the assurances she seeks, she does not believe them. She kills her children to save them from a worse fate: 'I swear, there is no way that I shall leave / my boys among my enemies so they / can treat them with atrocity.'[72] It is interesting that it is the image of sexual frenzy that has most popularly attached itself to *Medea*, and that what gets lost in translation is any trace of the reasons a mother might have for thinking there is no longer any place in the world for her own children. Véronique Olmi's bestselling 2001 rewrite of *Medea* has the title *Bord de mer* (the translation *Beside the Sea* loses the pun *mer/mère*, by the sea/mother at the edge). Before murdering her two sons on a visit to the seaside, the mother goes quietly mad and dreams of spending her life in bed with her children watching the telly, 'holding on to the remote, we'd have switched the world off as soon as it fucked up.'[73] Across the centuries, like the *Oresteia*, Medea still speaks to us. 'Medea gets away with it,' writes Margaret Reynolds on the history of *Medea* in performance: 'That is why we love her . . . She allows us, if only for the length of her performance, the freedom to perform ourselves – or, rather, the selves that we should be, if we were not bound by convention, by law, by order and decree.'[74]

But it is Christa Wolf's 1996 retelling that is, for me, the strongest act of reclamation and the true feminist text. In this version, Medea does not kill her children, nor Creon's daughter Glauce, nor her brother Absyrtus, who, in another strand of the legend, she murdered before fleeing her original home of Colchis with Jason. If all this is laid at her door by the citizens of Corinth it is because she has uncovered that city's grotesque secret, the murder of Glauce's sister by Creon in order to keep his succession out of the grasp of his wife, who after the killing goes silent and progressively mad (likewise, it is Medea's father who had murdered Absyrtus, whom he saw as a rival for the succession). 'Either I'm out of my mind,' Medea muses in her first soliloquy, 'or their city is founded on a crime.'[75] This makes Medea into a psychoanalyst – the allusions are explicit – as she slowly persuades the ailing Glauce that she knows the truth, saw the deed. Medea taught her, Glauce reflects, that 'there is no thought I must forbid myself to have.'[76]

Above all, Medea's true crime is to shatter a myth of collective innocence. She is a scapegoat, another mother who is guilty because everyone else has failed: 'They're looking for a woman who will tell them they are not guilty of anything.'[77] Worse, by exposing the crime she risks plunging the whole nation into sorrow: 'Someone must grieve.'[78] Remember Adrienne Rich: 'We know too much at first hand [of] the violence which over centuries we have been told is the way of the world, but which we exist to mitigate and assuage.'[79] In Wolf's version, it is because Medea assuages nothing that she is indicted of all crimes. It is because she knows that the city is built on the corpses of children that she is hounded out of Corinth. Wolf has used her *Medea* to write a parable of Germany in the twentieth century – in *On the Natural History of Destruction*, his account of the silence that followed the Allied bombing of German cities at the end of the Second World War, W. G. Sebald writes of the 'well-kept secret of the corpses built into the foundations of our state'.[80] Above all, she has turned Medea into a story of what happens when a woman is held responsible for the ills of the world. 'She [Medea] has no need of our doubt, of our endeavours to do her justice,' Wolf writes in her prelude. 'We must venture into the darkest core of our misjudgement – of her and of ourselves – simply walk in, with one another, behind one another, while the crash of collapsing walls sounds in our ears.'[81]

2

PSYCHIC BLINDNESS

LOVING

Matilda the Musical, adapted from Roald Dahl's novel, opens with what might be described as the paradox of maternal recognition. A troupe of hideously grimacing children sing 'My mummy says I'm a miracle' in such a way as to suggest that they are monsters; meanwhile, Matilda, who really is miraculous in so far as she has magic powers, fails to be recognised or understood by her parents. Her mother, unaware she was pregnant more or less up to the point of delivery, clearly neither wanted nor knew what to do with a baby. Her father was expecting a boy (he persists in calling Matilda 'boy' until almost the end of the musical). They both hate their daughter for her gifts, and have nothing but contempt for the love of reading into which she pours her unhappiness and through which she escapes it. Matilda is special, we are repeatedly told. She needs to be seen. She is eventually adopted by a schoolteacher, Jenny Honey, who recognises her unique qualities – Jenny is an orphan, her mother died in childbirth (in the book, when she was two). The implication is that Jenny can save Matilda because she herself was denied, and therefore knows what it is that Matilda is looking for. Failed mothers are everywhere – overinvested, neglectful, dead. Just how high the stakes are can be gauged by the immense difficulty Dahl had in completing his story. In the first version, Matilda herself did not survive.

In the book, Dahl makes a point of stating which of these forms of parental failure is worst: parents 'who take no interest in their children . . . of course are far worse than the doting ones', although the venom he directs at the latter is pretty intense.[1] What is apparent, however, is that to be seen by a mother is a mixed blessing, to say the least. Too much and you will be a monster, not enough and the chances are you will also enter a not fully human world. It is the genius of Dahl's story to make something very difficult and very strange – Matilda is nothing if not strange – seem easy and obvious. A mother, as most writing on mothers seems to concur, must be there for her baby. This process will only kick in if she recognises the baby as her own, but not as 'His Majesty the Baby', to use Freud's formula, not as a narcissistic object, a mirror that perfectly reflects her own ideal image back to herself ('My mummy says I'm a miracle'). Instead, her task is to recognise who the baby is for her or himself, even though what that might mean is something neither of them can possibly know in advance. Such uncertainty is, it seems, hard to tolerate. Perhaps that is why 'His Majesty the Baby' continues to wield such power. After the birth of

Prince George in July 2013, the UK was given a more or less daily dose during the grand royal tour in April the following year, as the infant was credited, among other things, with having quelled any remnants of Republicanism in Australia. Proffered as a role model for mothers all over the world, the Duchess of Cambridge must also turn her firstborn into a king. The challenge will be to stop him becoming a monster or a nobody (or, most likely, a bit of both).

My question in this chapter is: what is being asked of mothers when they are expected to pour undiluted love and devotion into their child? I have called this section 'Loving', but it comes in a chapter with the title 'Psychic Blindness', which should provide a hint ('Love as Perversion' could have been another title for what follows). After all, whenever love is expected or demanded of anybody, we can be pretty sure that love is the last thing being talked about. Like the injunction to be spontaneous, a state that can only arise unbidden, the demand to love crushes its object and obliterates itself.

Expecting mothers to be perfect is, of course, not unrelated to the drive to perfection of the so-called 'overinvested' or 'narcissistic' mother, who sees the whole world – a world that must be flawless – in her baby. Or to put it another way, if you are asking mothers to be perfect, why wouldn't they pass that impossible demand on to their child? Any mother who obeys this diktat could therefore be said to be perversely fulfilling the requirements of her role. Perfection breeds perfection, lives frozen at the core, compulsively fawning over themselves (it is surely no coincidence that perfection is also the false promise of consumer objects, which is why every disappointing purchase leads to the next).

Once again, Dahl's hideous, miraculous children serve to make a profound point. Bringing up a child to believe it is a miracle is not an act of love but a form of cruelty, even if at the opposite pole from that of neglect. How can such a child find a place in the world, since the only person they will be able to see will be themselves? This is the opposite of saying that all children are miracles, a proposition that recognises each child as unique while placing every single child in the world on a par with each other. Nor does it have anything to do with the wonder that can fall on a mother in relation to her newborn child, what the British child psychoanalyst and paediatrician D. W. Winnicott, and many psychoanalysts after him, term 'primary maternal preoccupation', which refers to the form of all-absorbing attention that a mother, in the very earliest stages, bestows on her baby. This may be something many mothers recognise without accepting its punishing intensifier, the version of motherhood into which it is often so effortlessly folded: a mother must live only for her child, a mother is a mother and nothing else.

The question then becomes how to acknowledge a new birth as the event that it is, without immediately divesting the newborn of its humanity. 'Every infant born,' writes Adrienne Rich, to quote again from *Of Woman Born*, 'is testimony to the intricacy and breadth of possibilities inherent in humanity.'[2] The rest of her book relentlessly charts how far motherhood as institution crushes that dream. For Hannah Arendt, in a passage Rich seems to be partly evoking, every new birth is the supreme anti-totalitarian moment. In Arendt's view, freedom is identical with the capacity to begin. Over such beginnings, she writes, 'no logic, no cogent deduction can have any power because the chain presupposes, in the form of a premise, a new beginning.'[3] Totalitarian terror is therefore needed, 'lest with the birth of each new human being a new beginning arise and raise its voice in the world'.[4]

In *The Years*, written on the eve of German fascism, Virginia Woolf treads similar ground. She is commenting on the dire consequences of parental exclusivity, on the damage it does to the social fabric – which was on the point of being rent beyond repair – to think it right to put your child, your family, before everyone else. She is also suggesting that, while England takes pride in its difference from Nazi Germany, there might nonetheless be a link between the overweening egoism of the bourgeois family and the autocracy of statehood (a point central to *Three Guineas*, which she was writing at the same time). At a family gathering in the mid-1930s – this final section of the novel is called 'Present Day' – North, the now grown-up grandson of Colonel Pargiter, is observing people politely enquiring about each other's children: '*my* boy – *my* girl . . . they were saying. But they're not interested in other people's children, he observed. Only in their own; their own property; their own flesh and blood, which they would protect with the unsheathed claws of the primeval swamp, he thought . . . how then can we be civilised?'⁵ Protecting with unsheathed claws is an image commonly used to describe a mother lion with her cubs. In their different but connected ways, Rich, Arendt and Woolf are all describing how, at the centre of human nurture and in its name, the intricacy and breadth of human possibility can be sidelined or quashed before it has even begun. And the ones expected to fulfil this deadly template of absolute singular devotion and blindness – all under the guise of nourishing the world's future – are mothers.

Rachel Cusk's *A Life's Work*, mentioned in the last chapter, provides a visceral account of the complete loss of any sense of social personhood that followed the birth of her first baby (the book was much praised and much hated on its publication in 2001). But perhaps it is because she charts that collapse so bloodily that at the same time she can see how motherhood can also offer a heightened emotional link to the world's wider stage: 'In motherhood, I have experienced myself as both more virtuous and terrible, and more implicated too in the world's virtue and terror, than I could from the anonymity of childlessness have thought possible.'[6] Unlike some of the Greek women we saw in the last chapter, becoming a mother does not allow her to remain in the public arena (instead 'civilisation' takes on the aura of something 'vain and deathly').[7] But Cusk's insight can help us to see why any discourse that dwells solely on the virtue of mothers and motherhood is such a con, since, among other things, it is asking women to conspire in cutting off the world from self-knowledge.

If we are all capable of virtue and terror, then no one culture, certainly not Western culture, can claim a monopoly on virtue, and the capacity for terror cannot be conveniently projected onto everyone other than oneself. 'I do not see the mother with her child,' Rich writes, once more way ahead of the game, 'as either more morally credible or more morally capable than any other woman.'[8] 'I got depressed,' Mary-Kay Wilmers writes on the birth of her first son in 1972, 'because instead of maternal goodness welling up inside me, the situation seemed to open up new areas of badness in my character.'[9] (Hard not to conclude that the expectation of goodness played its part in provoking the depression in the first place.) Why should mothers, any more than anybody else, be good? We talk of a mother's suffocating love. But the one in danger of being smothered by love might not be the infant but, under the weight of such a demand, the mother.

Women who are mothers are not better or more

creative than women who are not. They have simply chosen to do things differently, to live other lives. For that reason, Denise Riley concluded in *War in the Nursery* (1983), her path-breaking study of maternal social policy after the Second World War, feminism has nothing to gain from any validation of motherhood in the name of female creativity or power.[10] This is not to say that motherhood cannot be experienced as creative or that being a mother does not give you another take on the world. It is simply to warn of the ease with which such an idea slips out of women's own grasp and into the instructive mode – 'Be good!' – a demand, an imperative, a trap. Women writers like Rich and Cusk, and also Luise Eichenbaum, Susie Orbach, Rozsika Parker and Lisa Baraitser, who have long insisted on the complex run of emotions to which motherhood gives rise, are issuing a type of political corrective, sourced in but far outreaching the domain of motherhood itself.[11]

Parker's book has the title *Torn in Two*, the one who is torn being, of course, the mother (as any mother will recognise). But there is another no less far-reaching implication. It is the demand to be one thing only – love and goodness incarnate – that is intolerable for any mother, and tears her mentally and physically to shreds. For it is perfectly possible to acknowledge that the love a mother may feel for her child is like no other, without buying into all the dire psychic trappings that are meant to follow. The idea of maternal virtue is a myth that serves no one, certainly not mothers, nor the world whose redemption it is meant to serve. Or to put it more simply, no woman who has ever been a mother can believe for a second that she is only ever nice (virtue *and* terror both).

We might also, perhaps scandalously, at least raise the question: who – mothers or non-mothers, parents or non-parents – loves children most? 'People who choose not to have children,' writes contemporary French philosopher Michel Onfray, 'love them just as much, if not more, than parents who are abundantly fruitful.' He continues:

> Asked why he had abstained from producing an heir, Thalès de Milet replied: 'Precisely because I love children . . . Who truly finds reality sufficiently desirable to introduce their son or daughter to the inevitability of death, to the treachery of man's dealing with man, to the self-interest that fuels the world, to the burden of being forced to do tiring work for pay, if not to precarious employment? How could parents be so naïve, stupid and short-sighted as to love misery, destitution, poverty, old age and misery enough to want to pass them on to their offspring? . . . Should we really use the word *love* to describe the transmission of such evils to flesh of our flesh?'[12]

You don't have to buy into this view of life, or the outdated, male-centric issue of an heir, to accept the validity of the question, especially on behalf of women who, in the name of love, are expected to be mothers. Mothers do not have a monopoly of love in the world, nor should it be asked of them. Anyone claiming such a monopoly is likely to be suffering from tunnel vision. Anyone trying to fulfil this demand will simply suffer. These are the partial tales of love, and they never ring true.

*

The supreme symbol of mother love is, of course, the breast, which reappears in modern discussions of motherhood having lost none of the punitive allure we saw in Ancient Greece (again, if anything it seems to have intensified). In *The Conflict: How Modern Motherhood Undermines the Status of Women*, Elisabeth Badinter, long-standing critic of twentieth-century Western ideologies of motherhood, argues that the position of mothers is getting worse.[13] In response to the economic crisis, and what she sees as a crisis of identity between the sexes, a new eco-maternalism, an updated ecological version of the maternal instinct as 'innate, essential, eternal, non-negotiable', in the words of one commentator, is driving many women back into the home (although French women come in for special praise for bucking the trend). Badinter blames a 'sacred alliance' of reactionaries and a new 'essentialist feminism' with Mother Nature at its core. Central to this project is breastfeeding. In

1956, La Leche League was formed by American mothers to promote breastfeeding. By 1981, the LLL, as it is known, had 17,000 trained group leaders; by 1990 its book, *The Womanly Art of Breastfeeding*, had sold over two million copies. According to Badinter, the breastfeeding rate in the US rose from 38 per cent in the late 1940s to 60 per cent by the mid-1980s, and reached 75 per cent by 2011.[14] 'I AM THE MILK OF YOUR BREASTS. YOU SHALL HAVE NO OTHER FORM OF INFANT NUTRITION IN YOUR HOUSE' was, according to Badinter, one of the pronouncements on the website Alternamoms, which takes its cue from the 'Ten Commandments' (*sic*) of the LLL (capitals original).[15]

In the 1980s, attachment parenting (or pure parenting, as it is also known) was founded by fundamentalist Christians William and Martha Sears, with an increasing following in the US and UK today. In fact, the UK breastfeeding rate was recently reported as the lowest in the world, with less than half of women still breastfeeding two months after the birth of their babies (when interviewed, women most often cited embarrassment at doing so in public as the main reason).[16] With a devotion to match LLL, attachment parenting recommends that breastfeeding be more or less non-stop. Mothers are instructed to devote themselves wholly to their babies, step off the career track, and as one journalist put it, 'subjugate yourself to your baby or else.'[17] The racial and class bias is glaring – such an option is hardly viable for a single Latina mother working in Walmart. As is the potential political manipulation – one member of the group suggested that the gay massacre carried out by Omar Mateen in Orlando in June 2016 was most likely attributable to negligent mothering when he was a child. 'Breastfeed or your child might become a mass murderer' – mothers once again answerable for just about everything (no mention of homophobia or gun control or the police as agents for the violence of the state).

Above all, whenever any aspect of mothering is vaunted as the emblem of health, love and devotion, you can be sure that a whole complex range of emotions, of what humans are capable of feeling, is being silenced or suppressed. Such injunctions wipe pleasure and pain, eros and death from the slate. Why, French psychoanalyst Jean Laplanche once mused, are there no artistic representations, or any recognition in psycho-analytic writing, of the erotic pleasure that a mother gains in breastfeeding her child? As if to say, breastfeeding is okay (indeed obligatory), but not so okay is its attendant pleasure. Remember Lysias' tale of the breast-feeding mother whose husband, if only he had clocked on to her sensuous enjoyment, would have known that she was bound to take a lover. I have known mothers who stopped breastfeeding simply because they felt they were liking it too much. I have also always thought that revulsion at such pleasure plays a huge part in campaigns to keep breastfeeding out of public spaces.

In award-winning poet Hollie McNish's video 'Embarrassed' – seven million views on the web – nursing mothers sit on toilet lids feeding their babies: 'For God's sake, Jesus drank it, and Siddhartha, Mohammed and Moses and both of their fathers, Ganesh and Shiva and Brigit and Buddha. I'm sure they weren't doing it sitting on shit, because their mothers sat embarrassed on cold toilet lids, in a country of billboards covered in tits.' As the video also points out, kids die from bottled milk in towns and cities drowning in pollution and sewage: 'and they [powder milk companies] know that they're doing it.' As McNish also makes clear, she is not instructing all mothers to breastfeed.[18]

For a counterexample to Laplanche's observation that there are few, if any, representations of a mother's pleasure, I would suggest the fifteenth-century Italian painter Liberale da Verona's depiction 'Sleeping Mother with a Child at Her Breast', which I was delighted to come across at the Albertina Collection in Vienna. It portrays a nursing mother, head thrown back, eyes half-closed, in a paroxysm of delight. The etching surely rivals Bernini's sculpture of St Teresa in Rome for the intensity with which it depicts the joy of female sexuality (St Teresa's ecstasy being, no less scandalously, proffered to the gods). In fact, depictions of a mother's erotic pleasure in breastfeeding are there to be found, but you have to go in search of them. This is a passage from Naomi Mitchison's 1931 novel *The Corn King and the Spring Queen*, sent to me by feminist literary critic Jan Montefiore, one of a run of communications I received when I first suggested such representations were rare. The heroine, Erif Der, is nursing her baby son:

> He began to give little panting, eager cries of desire for food and the warmth and tenderness that went with it. Erif's breasts answered to the noise with a pleasant hardening, a faint ache waiting to be assuaged . . . For a moment she teased him, withholding herself; then, as she felt the milk in her springing towards him, she let him settle, thrusting her breast deep into the hollow of his mouth, that seized on her with a rhythmic throb of acceptance, deep sucking of lips and tongue and cheeks . . . He lay across her belly and thighs, heavy and utterly alive.[19]

Laplanche was right about the classical psychoanalytic literature that tends to make erotic desire, in the mother–baby pair, almost exclusively the province of the infant (desexualising the mother, like everyone else). One exception is the analyst Helene Deutsch, who, writing at about the same time as Mitchison and to a similar tune, describes birth and after as a more or less continuous erotic exchange of bodily organs and pleasures. 'In coitus,' she writes with unerring assurance, 'the penis becomes the breast while in lactation the breast becomes the penis.' The mind boggles (although the image of Erif's hardening breasts comes close).[20] For the most part, however, the pleasure a mother might experience from a baby at the breast is either unspeakable or it makes her accessory to a crime.

There is, of course, not the slightest trace of any such pleasure – heaven forbid – in LLL or pure parenting. No less conspicuous, although perhaps slightly more predictable, is their complete silence on breastfeeding as a potential source of anxiety or pain. Not all mothers breastfeed, whether out of choice, or because it does not work, or because it is too painful (pleasure is only the half of it). The complexity of breastfeeding is another aspect of mothering that is rarely talked about – one result of the impoverished alternatives on offer of being 'for' or 'against'. 'Naturalness, spontaneity are the *mots d'ordre*' (marching orders, one might translate), Wilmers writes. 'Which hardly takes into account the fury one may oneself feel at an infant who rages when he should be feeding, and indeed would like to be feeding if only he could stop raging.'[21]

On Mother's Day 2014, Courtney Love opened her concert at the Shepherd's Bush Empire in London with: 'Happy Mother's Day. I got flowers for mine with a note saying, "Thanks for not breastfeeding."' She is the high priestess of breastfeeding, not as pure nature but as sensuous, potentially harrowing art:

'I'm eating you, I'm overfed
Your milk's in my mouth, it makes me sick.'

'And all your milk is sour
And I can only cry
And I can only cower
And I can only cry
You have all the power.'

'I want my baby, where is the baby
I want my baby, where is the baby
There is no milk
There is no milk.'

Those last lines are taken from a song entitled 'I Think That I Would Die'.[22] In this distraught rendering, milk gluts, sours, sickens; the mother is not feeding but eating her baby. We could not be further from the conventional image of breastfeeding, where, it is safely assumed, all body fluids are flowing in the right direction and land in the right place. This might be dismissed as extreme. And yet the body *in extremis* – the body experiencing itself acutely *as* a body – is a human reality to which mothers cannot help but have access, although once again they are expected to put a lid on it, to make everything sweet and nice. They can, they must, love, hold, coddle their babies, but on condition of warding off the danger of any spillages – blood, guts, misery and lust. Their task is to prevent such intensities from going too far, to clean out the drains, on behalf of everyone.

*

So how to tell the tales of love of and for mothers? Or, how to listen to the tales that mothers choose to tell? We have seen how, on this matter, the dominant language of the Western world has a tendency to be prissy (moralistic, sentimental, coercive, blind), as if the best to be hoped for is wrapping a mother and her baby in emotional cling film. A killing prospect, since if you leach out of a mother any but the most anodyne, saccharine feelings, there will be nobody or nothing left. And if you take a mother sitting (not prone, not enraptured) with her baby at her breast, eyes demurely focused on her infant, as the supreme image of mothering then you shrink her pleasure, her anxiety, her world. Perhaps most important of all, if you ignore the more disturbing narratives that are there to be read, which must include the lengths a mother can be driven by love of her child, then you wipe whole histories from the map, shutting down – in the name of essence or nature or virtue – the complex tracks that can run across continents and time.

Toni Morrison's Pulitzer Prize-winning *Beloved* (1987) tells the story of a woman who kills her baby rather than let her be captured and grow up into a life of slavery from which the mother has barely escaped.

Morrison has firmly stated that this is not the tale of
Medea retold: 'Sethe didn't do what Medea did and kill
her children because of some guy.'[23] There could be no
greater difference between killing your sons in a desperate rage and deciding, in an act of supreme care, that
a daughter is better off dead than sold into the slavery
that still haunts the mother. Although in one reading of
Medea she does indeed kill her children to save them
from a worse fate (in several others she does not kill
them at all).

Sethe kills her daughter out of love. One of the most
powerful aspects of this novel is the way it shows, again
without sentimentality, how it can be an act of human
responsibility for a mother to take the unspeakable
action which historically she has to take – although she
is crucially also her own agent – at the same time as
she knows in every bone and beaten scar on her body
that her action resolves nothing, that the after-effects of
our choices stay with us for ever (Beloved returns as a
ghost). Morrison is extending the scope of mothering
across the broadest, and most incriminating, sweep of
history. She is telling her white readers – she said she
wrote the novel to lift the lid on America's suppressed
history of slavery – that in an inhuman world a mother
can only be a mother in so far as history permits, which
might mean killing your child. When Sethe first recognises the face of her returned dead daughter, she has to
rush around the side of her house to empty her bladder,

an 'unmanageable' emergency she had not experienced since she herself was a young girl. In this radical and brilliantly counter-intuitive moment, Morrison answers in one fell swoop the nursery dictators and fanatics of mothering from now and yesteryear for whom the only liquid that can acceptably pour out of a mother's body is milk.[24]

Once again, the ultimate sin is pleasure, and how it is regulated is the surest measure of oppression: 'Slaves not supposed to have pleasurable feelings on their own,' Beloved's sister Denver reflects, 'their bodies not supposed to be like that, but they have to have as many children as they can to please whoever owned them. Still, they were not supposed to have pleasure deep down. [Grandma Suggs] said for me not to listen to all that. That I should always listen to my body and love it.'[25] Obligatory childbearing, no bodily pleasure, no self-love (for which love of a child is so often decreed as the substitute) – this is the slave-owning version of motherhood. Morrison is drawing up to the surface a historical reality that hugely exceeds the true story of Margaret Garner, on which her novel was based.[26] Scrape the surface of this history and you find that many slave women made the choice not to preserve the lives of their children (among whom the infant mortality rate was in any case high). Ally, the slave of one George Miller in Fairfax County, Virginia, in 1835, Polley in Buckingham County in 1818, and Kesiah in 1834, were all convicted for killing their infants, and each one was sentenced to hang for her crime. In 1815, at the trial of Hannah, a slave from Granville County, North Carolina, one witness testified that she had cut her child's throat and then attempted to slit her own.

On occasion a slave woman would use infanticide as a threat. In one example, which achieved some notoriety, a mother, faced with the prospect of being separated from her infant for some petty offence, held the baby by its feet in the air as if to smash its head onto the ground (the slave owner relented). Like abortion, infanticide was the harshest way of asserting autonomy, an answer to the inhospitality of the world. But it was no less an act 'taken in the interests of mothering': 'they made mothering decisions – decisions not to mother' (the words of Stephanie Shaw, from whose essay on slave mothers in the antebellum South I take these examples).[27] And, of course, breast milk was stolen. Slave women were often forced to feed the babies of their owners, their life – the life owing to their own children, whether alive or dead – mercilessly pumped into the suckled future of the oppressor (infants who as yet would have not the faintest idea of the disparity of their world from that of the nurturer at whose breast they were satiating themselves).

Some slave mothers tried to prepare their offspring for a life of freedom, but, for the most part, mothers whose children remained alive saw their main task as teaching them the skills of survival. Under such conditions,

mother love, as it is understood in white Western culture, is a luxury – this high-risk version of motherhood
has to be prescient and crafty rather than mollycoddled
and safe. 'Mothers may have ensured their daughters'
survival at the high cost of their emotional destruction,'
Patricia Hill Collins writes. 'On the other hand,' she continues, in words that have lost none of their pertinence
today, 'black daughters who offer serious challenges
to oppressive situations may not physically survive.'[28]
She was writing in the 1990s, long before the increased
racialised US state violence that precipitated Black Lives
Matter, and way before the election of Donald Trump in
November 2016 threatened to make the lives of blacks
in America, and indeed the world over, so much less safe.

Another example, this time from South Africa, tells
a different but not unrelated tale. In the first story of
her 1991 collection, *Living, Loving and Lying Awake
at Night*, Sindiwe Magona gives one of the most powerful renderings of what it means to abandon a child
out of love in the conditions of rampant, violent racial
inequality that prevailed under apartheid. She is the sole
provider for her five children – each one conceived on
her husband's return from his eleven-month stints in the
gold mines of Johannesburg, from where he no longer
sends her money: 'a dog that unsheathes itself onto a
tuft of grass. He forgot the grass he'd peed on.'[29] Five is
the number of children who remain: 'Had all her pregnancies come to fruition, and had none of her babies

died in infancy, there would have been perhaps double that number.'[30] Still nursing the youngest of her infants, she slips away in the night in search of work in a white 'madam's' house where she knows – as the rest of the stories confirm – she will be insulted, abused, exploited. 'The only way she could be a mother to her children would be to leave them' (the free indirect tense places the reader right inside her mind, leaving no room for dissent).[31]

But it is the fraught sensuality and wretched lyricism of the writing that makes this story so compelling and haunting, giving her readers a type of distorted permission to savour the cruel experience – as if, by mothering the language, Magona could partly compensate for her character's distress in leaving her children behind: 'She rose and stood still and straight as a reed on her mat while her thoughts galloped away'; 'The woman listened and imagined she heard: mmhh, psshh, mmhh-psshh; and could almost see the rise and fall of the baby's heaving form'; 'Light as dandelion seed adrift in April's breeze she walked away from the hut where her children slept.'[32] The climax comes when, bleeding from a thorn, imagining her six-month-old baby bursting her lungs for food, she stops to express the milk from her breasts:

Kneeling, she took out first the one, then the other breast. Plumped hard and veined, they were hot to her crying hand. Squirt-squirt; jets of white streamed to foam the ground. Squirt-squirt-squirt: the greedy soil quenched its thirst with her baby's life while near her knees the woman's eyes wet a spot.[33]

Not for one second does she hesitate on her path. 'One last sigh for the children who sent her away' – note it is the children sending her – 'How she loved them.' This is another kind of loving, stripped of any shred of sentimentality, witness to an injustice that it is now up to society to redress – the collection appeared three years before the end of apartheid. In these stories of mother love pushed to the limit, as told by Morrison and Magona, motherhood is not stranded on the far shore of history (as if a baby could suckle everything that she or he, and the whole wide world, needs from a mother's breast). Nor, by any stretch of the imagination, could you possibly believe that the solution to the ills charted by these writers without apology could ever arise solely out of motherhood itself.

*

The mothers of the Western world are at once punished for being mothers and instructed to love without reserve. The hate, we could say, is perfectly proportionate to the love, the intensity of the demand matches the deluded expectation, the veneration a cover for reproach. It is not to the tales of historic violence and abandonment by writers like Morrison and Magona that we should, therefore, turn for testimonies of the perversion of mother love in modern times. Instead, in the last part of this chapter, we should look deep inside the Western literary canon, where we find, in relation to motherhood, the most profound and heart-wrenching diagnosis and lament. When I came across by chance Edith Wharton's *The Mother's Recompense*, it felt as if it had fallen into my lap through the sheer force with which it brandishes in the reader's face a contemporary myth of motherhood as she takes to pieces the insanity that passes for normal in the world of white metropolitan elites of the last century, and still in many ways now.

The novel was published in 1925, nearly half a century before the feminism of the 1960s and 1970s made the impossible ideal of motherhood the target of critique. Little known today, yet it sold almost as many copies as *The Age of Innocence* and *The House of Mirth*, for which Wharton is most famous, competing with *The Great Gatsby* as a bestseller, and making its author $55,000 within a matter of months. In the year it was published, Wharton became the first woman to be awarded the gold medal of the National Institute of Arts and Letters. She was apparently offended to have her novel unfavourably described as 'old-fashioned' compared with the 'brilliant experimentalism' of Woolf's *Mrs Dalloway*, which was published in the same year.[34] It is true that *The Mother's Recompense* is written in a more traditional prose style.

Nonetheless, old-fashioned is a strange way to describe a novel in which a mother's love for her daughter brings both their lives to the brink of ruin.

Kate Clephane is a mother who abandons her daughter, Anne, but not out of harsh material necessity, far from it, as she is a wealthy New York socialite who decides she has to escape a stifling marriage to a controlling husband at any price. For several years she has tried in vain to adapt to his point of view, to her mother-in-law's exacting standards and 'to all the unintelligible ritual with which they barricaded themselves against the alarming business of living'.[35] The abandonment is not therefore casual. She acts out of despair (again it will take feminism many years before it catches up with her to make the destruction of women by the so-called normal family one of its loudest refrains). At her mother-in-law's outraged instigation – backed by lawyers, judges, trustees, guardians, 'all the natural enemies of women' – she has been allowed no contact with her daughter since she left for France on the cusp of the new century.[36] These are the people who have the power to order her life. Years later this will still be the reality for many women who choose to leave the marital home. I once knew a woman who lost custody of her children in the early 1980s – all her friends, her advocates, were discouraged from testifying as character witnesses on her behalf in court because they were divorcees and/or lesbians.

Kate Clephane's predicament has an afterlife long

beyond the end of the First World War, where the novel begins, when the mother-in-law has died and she is summoned back to New York by her forgiving daughter, eighteen years after, as she puts it, she had lost her: '"lost" was the euphemism she had invented (as people called the Furies the Amiable Ones), because a mother couldn't confess, even to her most secret self, that she had willingly deserted her daughter.'[37] She returns to a heartless opulent world, whose characters merge into a 'collective American face', and who have been strangely comforted by a war that barely touches them.[38] Kate, like Wharton, was awarded a war medal for her work in France. The passing reference to the Eumenides, however – 'the Furies the Amiable Ones' – tells that we have entered the world of Greek tragedy. The Eumenides, we should remember, are powerless to save the mother from a pitiless fate.

If *The Mother's Recompense* is a tale of abandonment and retribution, it is no less the story of a mother love that turns suffocatingly on itself. Such love is an offspring of guilt. There is agony lurking at its core. A mother, this story suggests, is most likely to go in search of it only in so far as she feels she has already failed. How can anyone expect this all-encompassing love to save the world when it is on a doomed mission to save itself? The recompense of the title is therefore ironic and something of a decoy. Wharton lifted it straight from the identical title of Grace Aguilar's sentimental paean to a mother's love, published posthumously in 1851: 'There are many sorrows and many cares inseparable from maternal love,' the mother of Aguilar's book states with overweening piety, 'but they are forgotten, utterly forgotten, or only remembered to enhance the recompense that sweetly follows.'[39] Wharton's novel has a very different tale to tell. The epigraph – 'Desolation is a delicate thing' – is from Shelley's *Prometheus Unbound*, which, as Wharton's biographer Hermione Lee points out, leads in the poem to an image of sleepers who dream visions: 'And call the monster, Love / And wake, and find the shadow Pain.'[40] The idea that love might be shadowed by pain may seem a commonplace, but not to anyone who has been reading most discourse, certainly at the time Wharton was writing, on the topic of mothers.

It is obvious from the outset that no good can come from the love Kate is praying she will refind in her relationship with her daughter: 'Kate felt as if they were two parts of some delicate instrument which fitted together as perfectly as if they had never been disjoined – as if Anne were that other half of her life, the half she had dreamed of and never lived ... the perfection she had sought and missed' (the repetition 'perfectly', 'perfection' is already a giveaway).[41] If for a while it looks as though her dream might be realised, it is definitively shattered from the moment she discovers that her daughter is engaged to marry Chris Fenno, the young man from Baltimore with whom she herself had the most serious love affair of her life, after the man for whom she deserted husband and daughter turned out to be no more than a flashy man with a yacht. At this point, the world of soap opera meets that of Greek tragedy – one reason this is such a compulsively readable novel. She has never got over this affair. Having decided she cannot possibly tell her daughter the truth, she confronts her former lover in a failed attempt to end an engagement she believes must lead to catastrophe. 'Perfect love,' we are told in another line cited in the novel, 'casteth out fear.'[42] It appears not.

Critics have suggested that the plot stretches credulity; or worse, that the novel is the bitter, uncomprehending rant of a childless woman writer with a hostile relationship to her own mother. Wharton's mother forbad her from reading novels until she was married and showed no sympathy for her writing career. There is, of course, another way of seeing this: that, in taking on such a delicate, fraught topic for women from beyond the experience of her own life, Wharton has revealed the remarkable reach of her mind. Indeed, paradoxical or counter-intuitive as it may sound, it might well be that at this time it was only a childless woman who could grant herself permission to 'confess, even to her most secret self, that she had willingly deserted her daughter'. In this, Wharton confirms Rich's suggestion that without the testimonies of childless or 'unchilded' women, as she prefers to name them, we would all suffer from spiritual malnutrition.[43]

Either way, it is the unlikely plot of Wharton's novel that allows her fully to expose the dangers of the intimacy longed for by mother and daughter alike. With remarkable boldness, she probes the undertow of their proximity, refusing to shy away from its lurking shadow of incest (one rarely spoken reason why such proximity excites praise and censoriousness in equal measure). Incest, most obviously, in so far as mother and daughter are in love with the same man. But incest, too, in the overbearing, body-to-body eros that binds the mother and her daughter: 'It did not seem to her, at the moment, as if she and her child were two, but as if her whole self had passed into the young body pressed pleadingly against her . . . as if it were her own sobs that were shaking her daughter's body.'[44] Kate is frightened at the likeness of her love for Anne 'to that other isolated and devouring emotion which her love for Chris had been'.[45] 'It is not clear,' Hermione Lee comments, 'whether the "incest-element" is the mother's desire for her daughter, or her horror at the spectacle of her with her own lover.'[46] The point being that Kate herself struggles to make the distinction.

On this basis and without a trace of moral compunction, Wharton pitches the mother–daughter idyll, as it was meant to be, into sheer horror. Kate now faces a dilemma that is 'natural and unnatural', 'horrible, intolerable and unescapable' (like incest), a problem 'too deeply rooted in living fibres to be torn out without mortal hurt'. Similarly, Freud explained that there can be no quick fixes in the mind because you cannot pluck out the neurotic symptom without damaging the healthy tissue in which it is psychically embedded.[47] She has entered a 'mad phantasmagoria'.[48] As if to say, enter this zone of the heart and there is no rational limit to what you may then find: 'A dark fermentation boiled up into her brain; every thought and feeling was clogged with thick entangling memories . . . Jealous? Was she jealous of her daughter? Was she physically jealous? . . . Was that why she had felt from the first as if some incestuous horror hung between them? She did not know – it was impossible to analyse her anguish.'[49]

Kate comes close to suicide, dashing madly one night into the streets; while Anne – in the deluded belief that Chris has called off the engagement because of the dis-parity in their fortunes – tries and fails to persuade her mother to disinherit her: 'You want me to go on suffer-ing then? You want to kill me?'[50] At one point Kate is compared to a moth 'battering itself to death' against 'an implacable blaze'.[51] There can be no resolution. If Kate gets her way and stops the marriage, then how long before 'mother and daughter were left facing each other like two ghosts in a grey world of disenchantment?'[52] In the end, the wedding goes ahead, with Kate's agon-ised, reluctant acquiescence. In the carriage on the way to the ceremony, she wishes her daughter all the happi-ness there ever was in the world 'beyond all imagining':

'"Oh, mother, take care!" Anne retorts, "Not too much! You frighten me."'[53]

Too much binding closeness, even – especially – between a mother and daughter, is killing (mother love with a vengeance). Under the veneer of civilisation, Wharton unpicks the fabric of a cliché, exposing the dangerous impulses for which such love – still idealised today – can act as both vehicle and cover. At the end of the novel, the mother's only recompense is the moral strength she gains from leaving once more for France and renouncing everything. Resolute and thoughtful, she is nonetheless, as Wharton makes a point of telling us, cut off from any trace of saving knowledge (her anguish is impossible for her 'to analyse'). But what mother in this place, at this time, had the tools to transform the historic cruelties of a world barely out of the war, or her own predicament, into understanding?

*

A century later, journalist Ariel Leve picks up the thread and writes her memoir of her mother – *An Abbreviated Life*, published in 2016 – from the other side of intimacy and neglect. Leve's mother doesn't exactly abandon her daughter, but she is a mother with whom the daughter has never spent a single full day of her life (eternal broken promises are a refrain). Nonetheless – for that very reason – she holds onto her daughter for dear life. When

Ariel used to come home from school as a young girl she would often find her mother naked in bed, from where she would summon her daughter to re-create 'The Happiest Day of My Life'. Ariel, and on one occasion a friend who had accompanied her home, would be expected to undress, curl up in a foetal position against her mother's body, her mother would pretend to push her out from her vagina and she would crawl out between her legs (the friend, who went home and promptly told her own mother, never visited again).

This is another tale of a New York socialite that delves into the psychopathology of an elite, self-preoccupied world, in this case the city's high artistic, bohemian life. Leve's mother, Sandra Hochman – never named in the book but not hard to identify – was a successful poet who surrounded herself with celebrities from the worlds of art and literature, filling her house with parties that kept her daughter awake at night throughout her school years. Easy to dismiss as perverse eccentricity or indeed sheer madness – impossible on the other hand for any reader not to weep with rage on this little girl's behalf – but then again not. Once again, this drama does not erupt out of nowhere. Motherhood without limits: in a twisted sense, Hochman is another mother who obeys this injunction to the letter. The more she neglects and manipulates her daughter, the more she calls absolute motherhood to her aid. Except that this time the story is told from the point of view of the daughter who charts

the damage with surgical precision: 'There were no barriers between what my mother was experiencing and
what I was exposed to. "We don't keep secrets from
each other" was a commandment. Nothing was ever
withheld.'[54] And with poetic eloquence (which is what
saves her): 'I had no choice but to exist in the sea that
she swam in. It was a fragile ecosystem where the tem-
perature changed without warning. My natural shape
was dissolved and I became shapeless. A plankton drifting in the current of her expectations.'[55]

Hochman is another mother weighed down by her
own guilt. But she does not know it. As a mother, she
never sees herself as anything but perfect. Her flagrant
narcissism, inseparable from her wilful passion for her
daughter, offers a beautiful illustration of the mind of a
mother in complete denial of itself. 'What did the real
damage was buried beneath the surface. Her denial that
these incidents [of neglect and inappropriate intimacy]
ever occurred and the accusation that I was looking to
punish her with my unjustified anger. The erasure of the
abuse was worse than the abuse.'[56] We do not get the
mother's story, and we should remember how easy it is
to blame the mother for all failings, but the daughter's
version receives ample confirmation from letters written
by Rita, her father's former girlfriend, who steps in to
care for her, as well as from the many others whom she
tracked down or discovered from her past in the course
of writing her book.

Leve has written a plea for understanding. She becomes a writer – like her mother, a debt she fully acknowledges – in order to purge damage she believes has been hard-wired into her brain. But she also knows that the trials of being a daughter of such a mother – of being a daughter, we might say – cannot be dispersed by a diktat of reason. Mario, the man with whom she has made a new life, is a diving teacher in Bali, as far away from the world she has lived in as could possibly be (no gadgets, few comforts, no rush, and often no words). Alongside the writing, it is Mario and his two daughters who give her the air to breathe. But even though he is a man of the sea, he finally has no patience with the waters – dissolving, drifting plankton and currents – she is swimming in: '"Why can't you just beat these demons and destroy them?"' he says to her, genuinely baffled. '"You mean, why can't I just get over it?" "Yes."' It's illogical to him that I would be a thinking person who can't control my thoughts. "Or if you can't get over it, then deal with it in a rational, sensible, way."'[57]

At one point in the book, Leve recounts coming across a poem by her mother in a collection about motherhood in a New York bookstore, which I was able to trace (try googling 'mothers and poetry' and see what you have to wade through: a mother's love is a gift, a true love, for ever). Like many of the others in the collection, 'Thoughts About My Daughter Before Sleep' is a love poem that could have, almost, been written by any mother: 'Ariel, one true / Miracle of my life, / I marvel to have made you perfect.' At least Sylvia Plath saved the name Ariel for the poem about her horse, whose wildness of spirit she was not therefore projecting onto, living or controlling through, her baby daughter. This is the last stanza of Hochman's poem, innocuous and clichéd enough, until it starts tipping, almost imperceptibly, into a more sinister zone:

> And through you
> I am born as I lie down
> In the seedbox of my own beginnings,
> Opening the wild part of me,
> Once lost, once lost
> As I was breathing
> In the vines of childhood

The mother finds her own wild, lost beginnings deep within the body of her daughter (which perhaps explains why this daughter will have to be endlessly reborn). The miracle – to return to where this chapter began – is the mother's doing alone: 'I marvel to have *made you perfect*,' a not so subtle rendering of the cry, 'You owe me everything,' which she also throws in her daughter's face. But, I find myself wondering, would these lines have given me the slightest pause had I not first read the daughter's chilling story?

You are born into the slipstream of your mother's

unconscious – as a therapist once said to me. No more so than in a culture that commands a mother to be all for her child. *An Abbreviated Life* is one more chapter in the cruel distortion of that command. We talk of the depths of attachment, but there can be no emancipation for mothers, no better life for the offspring of the future, unless we recognise what that seemingly innocent instruction – be all for your child – might mean. It should be clear by now that rational and sensible have very little to do with it, any more than controlling one's thoughts. Mario is not the first man, and will surely not be the last, to believe that all it takes is a bit of self-mastery to be able to walk away and leave the realm of mothers behind (as if, such impatience suggests, we could offload onto mothers the burden of the unconscious and then despatch mothers and unconscious together). But this, too, is a crippling vision – his mildly exasperated call to reason, issued in the imperative mode, the flip side of the mother's emotional hurricane. We have to look further. In most of the accounts of motherhood explored so far, something is missing or being pushed aside. Nothing less, I will now suggest, than a mother's right to know her own mind.

Against what, we might then ask, is all this the defence?
From the frenetic exhortations to breastfeed of the LLL
to the ostracism of the 'bad' mother, to the blinding
attachment that mothers are expected to invest in their
child? On behalf of what are all these pious, punitive
or simply dotty versions of motherhood – none of
which seem to be mutually exclusive – doing cover?
Elisabeth Badinter's *Mother Love*, her original critique
of the maternal instinct as inborn and universal, was
published in 1981 to a storm of controversy in France.
When her editor invited the renowned child psychoanalyst Bruno Bettelheim to contribute a preface, he
replied:

> I've spent my whole life working with children whose
> lives have been destroyed because their mothers hated
> them . . . Which demonstrates that there is no maternal
> instinct – of course there isn't . . . This book will only
> serve to free women from their feelings of guilt, the
> only restraint that means some children are saved from
> destruction, suicide, anorexia, etc. I don't want to give

my name to suppressing the last buttress that protects
a lot of unhappy children from destruction.[1]

The vitriol of this statement might take us close to the
heart of the matter. There is, he concurs, no maternal
instinct, which is why so many children are doomed (this
was before the revelations of how Bettelheim treated
the children in his care).[2] There is also, as we have seen
before, only the mother, no fathers and no hint of social
deprivation mentioned, which means outside the nursery
– the mother–baby bond – there is no world (it is therefore Bettelheim himself who tightens the maternal grip
on the baby). Only guilt, it seems, will secure a mother
to her child. Without such guilt, the child will not survive, although such an arrangement will scarcely make
the child happy: 'the last buttress that protects a lot of
unhappy children from destruction'.

Bettelheim has invented a kind of listen-with-mother
version of Freud's account of the superego, the agency
of social control in the mind that is meant to subdue
human desire but can only do so by strapping the poor,
defenceless ego to its allotted social role. For Freud,
the ferocity with which the superego carries out its
task means that we should acknowledge the oppressive
and self-defeating nature of civilisation's highest commands. The last thing psychoanalysis should do is join
in. Instead, if analysis can help reduce the harshness of
the superego, then you are less likely to go on punishing

others and yourself. For Bettelheim, on the other hand, mothers must be driven by guilt into a role that, by his own account, is false. Children must be saved from hatred at any price. And since he will not give his name to Badinter's book, even though he thinks she is right, the price includes suppressing the truth. Hatred is therefore the guilty party (something of a tautology). What is being asked of mothers – perhaps the demand behind all demands – is a hate-free world.

When D. W. Winnicott wrote his essay 'Hate in the Counter-Transference' in 1949, he surely must have known that he was breaking taboos. When he listed the eighteen reasons a mother has to hate her baby, he must have known that he was pushing hard against the ideal ('The mother hates the infant from the word go').[3] The last and most often cited in his list ('He excites her but frustrates – she mustn't eat him or trade in sex with him') is another of the rare instances in psychoanalytic writing where a mother is allowed to be sexually aroused by her baby.[4] Winnicott's essay has become a type of urtext for women seeking to shatter the cliché of benign, devoted motherhood, a weapon to be wielded on behalf of maternal ambivalence struggling to be recognised. Ambivalence does not, however, seem quite right to me, at least not as a set of feelings to be 'managed' or which contribute to the creativity of a mother's task, a reparative move often made in feminist discussions of maternal ambivalence, as if the only way to deal with maternal ambivalence is by giving it with one hand and taking it back with the other (which is oddly in tune with its nature).

In Winnicott's vocabulary, Melanie Klein's concept of reparation does not figure, a healing capacity that slowly develops in the infant in relation to the mother, and which allays the rage towards her – a rage inevitable for all babies as they encounter the earliest frustrations. He is talking about something else, something so acutely painful that it cannot be felt without the risk of effacing itself. It is a form of hatred that, against all her better 'instincts', the mother needs to know she is feeling, and to stay with, if the infant is to have any chance whatsoever of experiencing, other than by means of a violent ejection, true affect or feeling in her or himself. The alternative is masochism. Winnicott is therefore making a political point: 'If, for fear of what she may do, she cannot hate appropriately when hurt by her child she must fall back on masochism, and I think it is this that gives rise to the false theory of a natural masochism in women.'[5] The baby, he writes, 'needs hate to hate'.[6] Sentimentality, he concludes his paper, 'is useless for parents'.[7] This has lost none of its pertinence today. 'What we have, for the most part,' Daisy Waugh writes in *I Don't Know Why She Bothers: Guilt-Free Motherhood for Thoroughly Modern Women* (2013), 'is a repressive sentimentality, a smiling acceptance of female martyrdom, which teeters, at times, beyond martyrdom into a sort of approved, mass-culture masochism.'[8] Waugh's insights are, however, trounced by her breeziness – that 'Thoroughly Modern' of the title is the giveaway – with its suggestion that if mothers feel punished, they only have themselves to blame (guilt-free motherhood, when presented here as a mother's duty to herself, turns out to be no less punishing or guilt-inducing than the account of Bruno Bettelheim).

Winnicott's argument does not mean, as should not need stressing, that the mother does not love her baby. As Alison Bechdel puts it in her cartoon strip drama *Are You My Mother?*: 'The mother loves the baby too. But this is the point. Hate is a part of love.' Bechdel's book, published in 2012, narrates her quest to reach some kind of mutual recognition with her mother. Her bestselling *Fun Home* (2006), subtitled 'A Family Tragicomic', focused on her relationship with her father, the director of a funeral parlour – hence 'fun home' – who had homosexual relations, and at the age of forty-four committed suicide (as well as being turned into a Broadway musical that toured the US, *Fun Home* was removed from libraries in Missouri after local residents objected to its content). *Are You My Mother?* is a type of Winnicott primer. The chapter from which that quote is taken is called 'Hate', while others – 'True and False Self' and 'The Use of an Object' – are lifted straight from his writing. She tells us Winnicott's life story, lays out his eighteen reasons on the page, reminding us that he was

revolutionary for using 'he or she' and 'his or her' decades before anyone else. She also graphically pursues
him into the bedroom of his second marriage, where he
and his wife discuss the strangeness of sex (Bechdel is
not alone in assuming that only this second marriage
was consummated). 'I want him', the narrator says at
one point during therapy, 'to be my mother.'[9]

As well as issuing an unprecedented emotional permission to mothers, 'Hate in the Counter-Transference'
should be compulsory reading for anyone involved with
today's government-sponsored rapid, short-term talking cures (cognitive behavioural therapy and the like).
Winnicott was addressing himself to psychoanalysts who
could not bear the strain of acutely disturbed patients.
Only an analyst in touch with 'his own fear and hatred'
will be of any use to such a patient, only such an analyst will be responding to the patient's – as opposed to
the analyst's – own needs. CBT, with its questionnaires
and instant results, would then be therapy designed to
protect the therapist, by getting hatred out of the room
as fast as it can. For Winnicott, the analyst must place
her or himself 'in the position of the mother of an infant
unborn or newly born'.[10] This is not, in my understanding, how most analysts tend to think of themselves,
although Michael Balint's idea of analysis as fostering
the birth of a 'new beginning' gets close (an idea of birth
that has nothing to do, therefore, with the favourite
game of Ariel Leve's mother). Remember, too, Rich from

the start of this chapter: 'Every infant born is testimony to the intricacy and breadth of possibilities inherent in humanity.'[11] When Winnicott's widow was faced with the suggestion that Freud had admired Attila the Hun, she replied that he had also loved Virginia Woolf's focus on the 'intricate things' of life. 'I put the odds on a psychic death-match between Attila the Hun and Virginia Woolf at fifty-fifty,' Bechdel writes in response. 'To be a subject,' she continues, 'is an act of aggression.'[12] Violence, as any mother will tell you, is not something that can be lifted or erased from the human heart.

Winnicott is presenting us with a choice, one no less starkly on offer today. We can go for the therapeutic quick fix, the full-frontal assault on any traces of psychic complexity, to be smoked out like rats in the basement. We can opt for hatred of hatred (Bettelheim's problem, I would say). Or instead we can take as a model for our social as well as psychological well-being the complex, often painful reality of motherhood. This is not quite the same as suggesting mothers should rule the world, but it is close. Provided we hold on to the idea that what qualifies mothers for this task is that they are not in flight from the anguish of what it means to be human. Not, it also should be stated, that mothers are the only ones who ever have access to such insight.

*

Are You My Mother? is full of writers. Alongside Winnicott, they are mostly but not exclusively women, some of whom we have already come across: Rich, Woolf and Plath. *Are You My Mother?* is a textual collage. It is through fierce verbal and textual contestation that the narrator's struggle with her mother takes place: 'Language was our field of contest.'[13] When Bechdel was eleven, her mother 'took over' writing her diary entries on the eve of Rosh Hashanah: the day 'when the deeds of humanity are open for review', 'the righteous are inscribed' and 'the wicked blotted out' (she does not appear to see a problem in her mother thus assigning herself the place of divine writ and punishment).[14]

Her mother is a dedicated reader who took a master's degree in English education in order to qualify as a teacher, and who was also an amateur actress. As a young woman, she had attended *Roe v. Wade* demonstrations in support of abortion rights (although the ruling has repeatedly been subject to legal challenge and local bypass, when Bechdel wrote her book it was not threatened as today by the election of Trump). None of this means, however, that she can tolerate her daughter's lesbianism. When her daughter plucks up the courage at university to write and tell her, she replies: 'Couldn't you just get on with your work? You are young, you have talent, you have a mind?' This is an eerie echo of Mrs Winterson's riposte to the same revelation from Jeanette Winterson: 'Why be happy when you could be normal?' – the title of her justly celebrated memoir of 2011. The tragedy for Bechdel is that her mother cannot see the link between her daughter's right to mental freedom, no less the result of women's struggle, and her right to freedom in the sexual choices of her life. In fact, they are alternatives: 'you have a mind.'

Her mother suffered depression as a young woman. Psychoanalysis was not an option for her. We could say that psychoanalysis, like feminism – Bechdel is the child of both – came too late: 'By the time *The Feminine Mystique* was published in 1963, Mom was stuck at home with two small children.'[15] She is part of a generation, which is the generation of my own mother, whose destiny was above all to become mothers and who found themselves, after a devastating war, under the harshest obligation to be happy and fulfilled in that role. Could it be that however much they encouraged their own daughters' independence, however much they urged their daughters to live their own unlived lives, they were also silently obeying an injunction against experiencing the full range of their emotions? And that the demand they made on their daughters then became, above all else, to keep up that guard, to protect them from their own raging hearts?

Winnicott's 1949 essay would not, then, have arisen out of nowhere, but as a response to the suffocating psychic legacy the recent war was in danger of passing on to its children. For, to stay inside his vocabulary, the child of such a mother will be a false self, compliant not just with her mother's demands to do what the mother wants – which is how he mostly describes it – but with the mother's hidden inner world, a world of cloying, restricted vision, inside which she is flailing without knowing it. Unless the daughter manages to shatter the carapace that encases her in the mental space of a mother who, through no fault of her own, was never given the chance to understand her own mettle, to realise what – in all senses of the term – she was truly made of. Bechdel's answer to her own question – *Are You My Mother?* – is finally affirmative. But the path to understanding is littered with images, lifted from her dreams and nightmares, of cracking ice, shattered glass and kicked-in walls. 'It only occurs to me now as I am writing this book about my mother,' she muses as she lies, after one of her mishaps, with a patch over one eye, 'that perhaps I had scratched my cornea to punish myself for "seeing" the truth about my family.'[16] This also adds another dimension to Bechdel's choice to be a graphic artist (to make us *see*).

Perhaps we should be asking a slightly different question – not what a mother is or should be, but what version of motherhood might make it possible for a mother to listen to her child? For if Western culture in our times, especially in the US and Europe, has repeatedly conspired to silence the inner life of the mother by laying on mothers the heaviest weight of its own impossible and most punishing ideals, and if the term 'mothers' is so often a trigger for a willed self-perfection that crushes women as mothers before anyone else, then how can they be expected to hear their children's cry – not as in wailing babies, which is of course hard enough – but as protest and plaint? How can they bear to watch their child shed the yoke of false mental safety, turning what was meant to be the psychic legacy of their own version of motherhood on its head?

For me, this has always been the best way to think about the relationship between Sylvia Plath and her mother, which is not quite the same as focusing on the excessive closeness or osmosis through which that relationship has often been analysed. In *Are You My Mother?* Bechdel reads Woolf but not Plath, her mother more or less the reverse (as if, between mother and daughter at least, the one has to exclude the other). This leaves a chasm between these two preferred writers, notably on the subject of mothers. In fact, Plath's 1962 verse drama, *Three Women – A Poem for Three Voices*, her voice meditation on three women in a maternity ward, was inspired by Woolf's *The Waves*.[17] When Plath's mother, Aurelia, lectured on her daughter after her death, she interspersed her memory of Sylvia with lines from the First Voice, the only one who ends up with her baby – the Second Voice miscarries, the Third Voice abandons her newborn child. When the BBC issued the script in 1968, they named this First Voice 'Wife', the two others, 'Secretary' and 'Girl', a gross interference, since in the text only the woman who miscarries is represented as having a husband (if you have a baby, you must be a wife). From out of the modulated confusion of the three voices, which is the genius of Plath's poem – a community of mothers whose voices gradually merge across divisions of experience, domestic life and class – Aurelia Plath lifts and isolates lines like these from the First Voice:

> What did my fingers do before they held him?
> What did my heart do with its love?

And these:

> I shall meditate upon normality.
> I shall meditate upon my little son.
> . . .
> I do not will him to be exceptional.
> It is the exception that interests the devil.

She left out lines like these:

> There is no miracle more cruel than this.
> . . .
> I am the centre of an atrocity.
> What pains, what sorrowing must I be mothering?
> Can such innocence kill and kill? It milks my life.

> I am breaking apart like the world.[18]

The point being that Plath did not shy from putting atrocity, cruelty and murderousness in the midst of a mother's love: 'The world conceives / Its end and runs towards it, arms held out in love.'[19] But her own mother could not stand it. A mother censors a daughter's representation of mothering, shutting down the world of thought. 'Don't talk to me about the world needing cheerful stuff!' Plath wrote to her mother in her last letters, 'stop trying to get me to write about "decent, courageous people" – read the *Ladies Home Journal* for those.'[20] The last thing a young mother needs, I hear Plath saying, is false decency, courage and cheer (a perfect definition of a compliant self). If it was just a question of cramping her daughter's style, then, however poignant this story, it would be easy to point to the blindness of Plath's mother and turn away. But the implications surely reach beyond the tragedy of this famous case. What on earth do we expect, as long as society continues to believe it has the right to trample over the mental lives of mothers?

*

For the most part, the world, like Aurelia Plath, does not want to know about this dark underside of loving – instead projecting onto the minds and bodies of mothers a revulsion for the complexities of the human mind. The more I have read, the more motherhood has started to feel like a ball tossed from one end of a playing field to the other, or perhaps more like the net stretched taut across a tennis court, which the frenzied players, hitting the ball as hard and fast as they can, must avoid touching at any cost (although it determines their every move). Or, to draw on set theory, a very different field of reference, we could say that a mother is the set of all possible sets, the one all-embracing set that contains everything, including itself. Mothers, of course, are classically thought of as containers, the Greek idea of the womb as a purely passive receptacle being perhaps the most egregious version of them all. But that a mother contains is surely true: inside her body and then again when she holds her baby. In one psychoanalytic model, it then also falls to her to contain all the overwhelming impulses the baby cannot contain or manage on its own behalf – which is why a mother who pushes away difficult feelings, too eager to turn away from pain and rage to decency and cheer, is useless.

Nor are these impulses simply the result of the dissatisfactions of life that all humans, in the course of development, find themselves up against. 'Even the most loving mother,' Melanie Klein writes at the end of her 1963 essay on the *Oresteia*, 'cannot satisfy the infant's most powerful emotional needs.' And, she continues, 'no reality situation can fulfil the often contradictory urges and wishes of the child's phantasy life.'[21] This means that in the beginning no one is guilty (even though Klein's dramatic account of the ferment of a baby's mind had critics accusing her of inserting into psychoanalysis the idea of original sin). There will always be something that escapes the remit of what a mother and baby can be for each other. There will always be a limit to what mothers can do for their child, and therefore – the unavoidable but mostly avoided consequence – to what we can ask of a mother.

'[It] is characteristic of the mental domain,' psychoanalyst W. R. Bion writes in his influential 1962 essay 'Container and Contained', that 'it cannot be contained within the framework of psychoanalytic theory' (a rare moment of psychoanalytic humility). Writing at almost exactly the same time, Klein and Bion are two psychoanalysts who alight on that aspect of the human mind that exceeds human grasp and which, for Bion at least, even psychoanalysis cannot be expected to hold in its proper place. 'I cannot observe Mr X,' Bion writes of one patient, 'because he will not remain "inside" the analytic situation or even "within" Mr X himself.' Mr X cannot be contained (he is spilling all over the place). Crucially for Bion, this is not just a matter of individual pathology but has wider social repercussions since it applies to any group trying to be 'respectable' (his word), to toe the line, to be 'anything in short, but *not* explosive'.[22] Not being explosive will do nicely as a definition of what is mostly asked of mothers, although, as any mother will testify, explosive is what she, to her utter dismay, often feels: there is nobody in the world I love as much as my child, nobody in the world who makes me as angry. It is this demand – to be respectable and unexplosive – that I see as most likely to drive mothers, and by extension their infants, crazy. I realise, of course, that this is the opposite of how these matters are normally thought about: if a mother cannot hold things together, who can?

Much follows from the blindness I am describing. Much about the experience of being a mother falls silently out of the public eye – since seeing oneself depends at least partly on being recognised by others – and out of the range of what many mothers can bear to know or think about themselves. The implications in the realm of social policy are profound, certainly in the UK and US, where the punishing expectations on mothers, especially in the teeth of social inequality, reach particularly gruelling heights. In 1998, Melissa Benn argued that post-feminism, 'self-contained to the point of arrogance', had slammed the lid back on the demands and painful emotions of motherhood that had been opened up by 1970s feminism (the wrong kind of containment, we might say).[23]

When Estela Welldon described as 'maternal perversion' the violent acts that some mothers commit against their children in *Mother, Madonna, Whore: The Idealization and Denigration of Motherhood* (1988), her book was banned in feminist bookshops. She was seen as blaming mothers for any damage to their children.

But Welldon's point was that refusal to acknowledge this 'dark side' of mothering meant abandoning such women to unacknowledged distress and their children to potential danger. No one, she observed, seemed to understand these women as mothers: '"women" were seen as capable of such actions, but not "mothers".'[24] Her book was therefore a plea for tolerance and understanding, although those terms are perhaps a bit soggy liberal when what is involved is more like dropping the scales from our eyes. For Welldon, a mother's perversion was the consequence of the abuse or neglect she will have suffered at the hands of her own mother, and most likely her mother's mother before her (a twisted version of Woolf's injunction to 'Think back through the grandmothers'). Instead of idealising and denigrating motherhood, social policy and psychological understanding need, therefore, to give motherhood its deserved but mostly refused place 'at the centre of human difficulty' (Juliet Mitchell in the foreword of the 1992 edition). Interestingly, the mothers in Welldon's study alternately idealised and cherished, then ravaged and discarded their children. Like the Stepford wives, robots who perform the patriarchal fantasy of the suburban wife to the letter, they were silently miming and reflecting back onto society the twin poles – unworldly expectation and rage – of its own inane, crippling vision, and treatment, of mothers.

Evidence suggests, especially in its dealings with such

hard cases, that social work is not immune to the same problem. Not least because social work as a profession is dominated by women, many of whom will be mothers themselves. 'Surprisingly little attention,' writes Brid Featherstone, professor of social work, 'has been paid to the fact that when mothers neglect, beat, suffocate, kill or sexually abuse their child/children, it is often another woman, who herself may be a mother and certainly has been a daughter, who is involved in investigating, assessing and working with her and her family.'[25] Whether as mother or daughter or both, a social worker is just as likely as anyone else to have been caught in the same emotional straitjacket, the same instructions as to what she must and must not feel (perhaps even more so, since entering one of the caring professions and taking care of other people's problems can also be a way of avoiding one's own).

A mother who admits to sexual desire for her own child can, for example, throw the whole professional network into disarray, especially when it is impossible to predict with any certainty whether such a mother is more or less likely to enact her feelings and actually abuse her child. The social worker listening to her may be appalled, but also find herself envying this woman's freedom to speak her mind. In one case, a social worker became enraged against a depressed mother who had asked for her son to be taken into care, finding herself denouncing her in the very language of stigma from which she thought herself immune and from which she should have been protecting her client, only to discover she was having her own fantasies of hitting the child: 'That a woman social worker might want to hit a child, particularly a vulnerable child who had been rejected by his mother, was quite literally unthinkable.'[26]

'What woman,' Adrienne Rich asks in the final chapter in *Of Woman Born* ('Violence: The Heart of Maternal Darkness'), 'has not dreamed of "going over the edge"?'[27] The chapter opens with the story of a mother who murdered two of her eight children in Chicago in 1974. This was the chapter Rich insisted on keeping in her book, despite the feminist requests for her to drop it. Perhaps the most radical, and for some unacceptable, thing about it was just this call for empathy: 'What woman has not . . . ?' to which 'What mother would dream of such a thing?' may well be the knee-jerk response. Instead, Rich is asking all women, wherever they find themselves, to make a leap of imagination into the life of a profoundly disturbed woman with too many children, not one of whom was wanted, stranded in a suburb of Chicago, with no household help or any respite, who was seen by her neighbours as the model of the devoted mother (Rich does suggest that, had help been on offer, she may well have refused to take it).

We must, she writes, reckon fully with the 'ambiguities of our being . . . with the potentialities for both creative and destructive energies in each of us' – words from the first edition that she reprints in italics in the preface to the later edition of her book.[28] She is issuing a cry for universal solidarity. She is asking women to see themselves in an act that most people, women, mothers – for good reason – cannot bear to contemplate. She is asking mothers to imagine, if only for a moment, that this dreadful story could have been their own. This is to enjoin on mothers a very specific ethical task, that of envisaging themselves as the person they would most hate to be. Never turn away – being socially inclusive follows from a willingness inside the heart to hold on, however painful, to everything. No mother is alien. We could not be further from where this book started – a world that finds it acceptable to turn back, and then target for special hatred, refugee mothers in flight from the attrition of their lives: 'Let them drown.'

*

She is the mother of all feminists, certainly from the mid-twentieth century in the West, one of the 'unchilded' women, to use Rich's phrase, without whom so many women would be suffering spiritual malnutrition. In de Beauvoir's eyes, becoming a mother is for a woman the most fundamental alienation of her freedom, certainly in the unequal world as it then was in the middle of the last century, and is still in so many ways today. For some 1970s feminists, partly taking, or thinking to take, their cue from her, not being a mother became a mantra: don't have children; if you do, pray for a girl, and whatever you do, make sure you bring up your child in a commune. To say that motherhood is, at moments, a hateful prospect for de Beauvoir is an understatement (although she never instructed women not to become mothers). But hate, as should be clear by now, is a form of energy, never so destructive for mothers, indeed for anyone, as when it is internally silenced or unthought. I end this chapter with Simone de Beauvoir, not just because her influence can be felt to this day but because she provides one of the strongest instances, in relation to mothers, of the generative force of antipathy.

De Beauvoir's image of motherhood suffers no piety. There is not the faintest chance she could be accused of promoting motherhood as ideal. She does not tell women how to be mothers (she does not tell women how to be anything). In de Beauvoir's writing, we can watch as motherhood is first measured against the goals of existential thought, key philosophy of the modern Western world, where it is found pitifully wanting. For existentialism, to be human is to craft the project of one's own life without impediment, a vision of existence that, it would be fair to say, could not be further from a mother's daily lived experience and world. But if motherhood is dismissed by de Beauvoir as an affront to a full life, it then bizarrely stages a comeback, carving a hole right through the heart of her philosophy. For all her antipathy, motherhood in de Beauvoir's thought takes us to the ethical crux of what being a mother might mean: both as a challenge to women's autonomy and as a potential opening to the widest, uncontrollable reach of what a human being is capable of.

When a woman becomes a mother, she loses her freedom. To this familiar plaint – versions of which have been scattered throughout this book – de Beauvoir adds her own unique dimension. A mother is deluded: 'alienated in her body and her social dignity'.[29] She thinks she has created the being growing inside her – in fact, her baby has no regard whatsoever for the body that gestates it: 'she does not really make the baby, the baby makes itself within her.'[30] This is not another version of the womb as passive receptacle; it is definitely not siding with the Greek story of fathers as sole generators of the embryo. But from the moment she conceives, a woman abdicates herself in favour of species being, she becomes part of a biological cycle over which she exerts no control. This reality 'devours' her; de Beauvoir thus neatly transposes to the felt experience of mothers an epithet – devouring mother – so often hurled against them.

In existential philosophy, the only viable existence is one that has achieved transcendence through its own activity. It is sheer degradation to be ruled by the contingencies of life. Giving birth, breastfeeding, even rearing children from infancy to adolescence, cannot be graced with the status of 'activities' (that would be news to most mothers). They engage no project – 'project' and 'activity' being key terms of self-affirmation in the existential lexicon.[31] 'A woman must choose,' de Beauvoir writes, 'between asserting her transcendence [as subject] and her alienation as an object.'[32] Her view of motherhood is a protest: 'the woman trapped in her home cannot found her existence for herself.'[33] It is also the logical effect of her philosophical intent: to make humans take the risk of freedom, and be fully accountable for the path they choose to forge through their lives. After all, it is indeed true that, if your vision of being in the world is one of untrammelled self-realisation, motherhood is a bit of a shock, to say the least. But that just might be, as de Beauvoir's account of mothering starts to suggest almost in spite of itself, because there is something wrong with the vision.

One is not born, one becomes a woman – her pronouncement is still seen as indispensable to feminism to this day: if you only become a woman, then what it means to be a woman becomes negotiable. Under the right political conditions, you can un-become her too, you can shed the requisite role and make yourself. Perhaps the sole exception to this truth of womanhood is that moment of blind necessity when, out of the body of a woman, something is being born. But if motherhood lashes you to species being, there is nonetheless always the danger that a mother will come to think of her baby as her doing, her creation, and, one short step, her property. She will expect too much of her child, in the belief that motherhood has endowed her life with meaning, ushering her into true being, which means in existential philosophy, conscious, sentient, being 'for itself'. Seen in this light, motherhood may foster the illusion of self-creation, a belief that the whole world pours, on command, out of ourselves. In fact, a baby is no more than a 'gratuitous proliferation' of brute matter whose 'pure contingency' is on a par with death.[34]

This sounds as bleak as can be. And yet, already we might see how this disquieting proposition might be turned, imaginatively, on its head. Having a baby brings a mother up against mortality. It puts her in touch with what, in every single human, cannot be self-fashioned or subdued to purpose. At the very moment a mother appears to be acquiring a new power she immediately has to cede it. She owns but does not own. She engenders a life only in so far as it escapes. The only question is whether this means a woman is better off not being a mother, although de Beauvoir never in fact says as much; or whether knowledge of this could instead open a path to what a mother might be (and not just on behalf of her baby or herself). De Beauvoir is clear that, in the present unequal social arrangements, organised by and to the advantage of men, mothers and their infants are under serious threat. A mother cannot secure the life of the child who is placed – sanctimoniously, thoughtlessly, mostly without material or practical support – in her total care: 'The great danger in which our way of life places the child, is that the mother to whom she or he is confined hand over foot is nearly always an unsatisfied woman . . . once we understand how far the present situation of women obstructs her fulfilment . . . we shudder that defenceless children are abandoned to her.'[35]

De Beauvoir's view of mothering as experience is not all dark. She talks of ecstasy, of some mothers' sense of fulfilment, of joy (a topic central in what follows here). In fact, alongside Winnicott, she deserves recognition as the first writer to speak out on maternal ambivalence (*The Second Sex* and his essay were published in the same year). Again on pregnancy:

> Pregnancy is a drama played out for the woman
> between self and self, one which she experiences both
> as enriching and as a mutilation: the foetus is part of
> her body, and at the same time a parasite exploiting
> her; she possesses, and is possessed by it; it contains
> her whole future and, bearing it inside herself, she
> feels as vast as the world; but this very richness
> annihilates her, and she feels she is nothing.[36]

De Beauvoir, indeed existential philosophy, is famously critical of psychoanalysis. From the outset, she insists that her vision of women's destiny, based on choice and freedom, is at odds with the psychoanalytic view of humans unconsciously driven and torn between conflicting desires.[37] But she also knows that becoming a mother is an experience that plunges a woman into the deepest recesses of herself. All mothers were once daughters. Whatever their situation, all mothers are likely to find themselves reliving at least fragments of their own experience as a child. In this domain of partly welcome, partly unwelcome involuntary recall, no woman – especially not in a world that effectively weds a mother to her daughter – is likely to be given an easy ride:

> It is when the little girl grows up that the true conflicts are born: we saw how she wants to assert her own autonomy against her mother: in her mother's eyes, this is the sign of hateful ingratitude; she sets herself against this will that escapes her; she cannot accept her double becoming *an other*. The pleasure tasted by men in relation to women: of feeling absolutely superior, a woman only ever feels in relation to her children, especially her daughters . . . Regardless of whether she is passionately enthused or hostile, the independence of her child is the ruin of her own hopes.[38]

How can a mother avoid the temptation to abuse her privileges, since to do so she would have to be either perfectly happy or a saint? What is a mother meant to do when confronted with the possibility of the child's own freedom – which must mean freedom from her mother?

Most likely, for de Beauvoir, she will resist with all her might, thereby repeating, although probably without knowing it, the worst of her own destiny in a patriarchal world. She becomes like a man – supreme irony – who uses woman as the means to his self-realisation. She has made the fatal mistake of thinking that she could create her own being on the back of someone else's (this is what a man is). As commentators have pointed out, de Beauvoir is clearly describing her struggles with her own mother – like Edith Wharton in the last chapter, de Beauvoir makes her bid for freedom out of a time of war. Like Wharton, she is charting the emotional history, the psychic fallout of a moment that laid an impossible injunction on women as mothers: be everything and nothing, be life and death for your child.

But if a mother is being asked for too much; if her daughter's freedom can only be asserted at the cost of her own; if life and death are joined in an interminable struggle at the core of her being, then the idea of pure, rational self-affirmation starts to look like a delusion. Caught between 'narcissism and altruism, dream, authenticity and bad faith, devotion and cynicism', being a mother is a 'strange compromise' (the inclusion of the dream suggests a condition suspended between the conscious and unconscious mind). Torn between these competing poles, how can motherhood be expected to contain itself? As it swerves from moment to moment, how can the experience of being a mother not act as a reminder of the fragile dispensation of hearts and minds and life? How many mothers find themselves thinking, even if without saying it out loud, that if they can only get through – if only they and their baby can survive – the next ten minutes or seconds, everything will be just fine (a claim, or plea, as urgent as it is frantic and mostly unheard)?

Motherhood is not knowledge or control. It may have to make non-stop decisions, but not according to some fatuous logic of mastery. If a mother struggling with her daughter is likely to find herself miming the worst of masculinity in a patriarchal world, at the same time she knows, de Beauvoir also tells us, that it falls to her as a mother to cede the limits of her own freedom. I remember my sister Gillian once saying when we were imagining a future as mothers, that, powerful women as we liked to see ourselves (we were barely in our twenties), once we became mothers we would have to know how to relinquish our power. She couldn't have been more right, although it is a source of endless sadness to me that she only knew me as a mother for less than a year before she died. What I think she was also saying is that the pleasure a mother takes in her child must be oblique, somewhat askew, if she is to avoid the trap of asking – from herself, from her child – too much. 'A mother who dreams of attaining through her child a fullness, warmth and value she has not managed to create for herself is headed for the greatest disappointment,' de Beauvoir writes. 'The child brings joy only to the woman who is capable of disinterestedly desiring the happiness of another, to one who without reversion to herself, seeks to go beyond her own experience.'[39] This is not masochism: you must suffer for your child. It is not a plea for altruism: always put your child first. It is a way of desiring the happiness of someone other – who happens to be your child – without placing that happiness in the service of your own ego (giving with one hand and taking back with the other). It is a way of being inhabited by the other. Despite de Beauvoir's objections, this would also be a very good working definition of the psychoanalytic unconscious.

At times, her account of motherhood as the bodily and mental subjugation of women is truly loathsome (as if a newly born could be the bad fairy at its own feast). But perhaps for that very reason, and long before the many writers on the deep ambivalence of motherhood to come, she was the first to delve into that complex space and call on us, via motherhood, to accept the alien in our midst, to make room, even if it brings the walls crashing down, for the stranger who lands on our shores. These ideas have had a feminist afterlife. Bulgarian-French thinker Julia Kristeva, who has influenced a whole later generation of feminists, follows a far more psychoanalytical path than de Beauvoir, but she joins her on this. To be a mother, to give birth, is to welcome a foreigner, which makes mothering simply 'the most intense form of contact with the strangeness of the one close to us and of ourselves' (which is why mothers are perhaps less likely to be fazed by the psychoanalytic belief that we are all radically strangers to ourselves).[40] 'In late August a baby was born,' Rivka Galchen writes in *Little Labours*, her 2016 account of new motherhood, 'or, as it seemed to me, a puma moved into my apartment, a near-mute force.'[41]

At the opposite pole of self-transcendence, light years from men subordinating women to that end, motherhood is presented by de Beauvoir, almost reluctantly, as an experience that places us on the path of a new ethics. Most simply, to be a mother, something has to give. It may sound obvious, but it is anything other than sentimental. Nor in the end does it compromise her demand for freedom for women, since to experience motherhood in this way, the mother must give herself freely to her child; though it does give the lie to the belief that you can truly be free all by yourself, or at anybody else's expense. If motherhood puts us in touch with the stranger, then we could not be further from the idea that 'my family' is the only one in the whole wide world that matters, the one I will fight for tooth and claw – to return to the corrupt and dementing version of mother love with which the first part of this chapter began ('How then can we be civilised?'). Today, women on the streets are taking up this challenge. In April 2017, ahead of 'Mother's Day', mothers, including the group MomsRising, marched on the Trump International Hotel in Washington with miniature statues of liberty to protest the administration's cruel immigration and deportation policy, and to demand it act with justice and compassion.

'The power of life,' Elena Ferrante writes, 'is damaged, humiliated by unjust modes of existence.'[42] It is not only motherhood that is impoverished if it fails to connect to the wider world; it is not only mothers and their children who are damaged and humiliated when their world, like a deadly flytrap, shuts in on itself. Today, in all of this, we should still be grateful to de Beauvoir for showing us just how high the stakes are. The question then becomes: what happens when a mother defies the instructions ringing in her ears and ventures down this strange, other path, trailing the debris of her heart and of everything around her as she goes? Where does it lead? What are the pleasures, the risks and the price? To explore these questions for our time, we now turn to Elena Ferrante, who offers her own brilliant, disconcerting reply.

3

THE AGONY AND THE ECSTASY

ELENA FERRANTE

She is one of the biggest European literary phenomena of the twenty-first century, but Elena Ferrante – by her own account – takes us back to the beginning, the world of the Greeks and Romans, one of the places where we started. 'I have to say,' she states in a *New York Times* interview in 2014, 'that I've never seen the classical world as an ancient world. Instead I feel its closeness.'[1] As a young girl, she would imagine the Bay of Naples peopled by sirens who spoke Greek. One of the relatively few pieces of biographical information she has volunteered is that she has a degree in classical literature, from which she learned 'many things about how to put words together'.[2] Medea and Dido are her heroines, the first for walking us into the unthinkable space of infanticide, the second for the civic and intimate generosity with which she set about building the city of Carthage: opening its doors (and her body) to a foreign exile, Aeneas, whatever tragic consequences in the end, and making sure that the temple of Juno, goddess of marriage and childbirth, should display the carnage of war, as a type of memento, on its walls.

Of these two women, Flaubert's Emma Bovary and Tolstoy's Anna Karenina are the diminished progeny, because they have lost 'the obscure force that pushed those heroines of the ancient world to use infanticide or suicide as rebellion or revenge or curse'.[3] They have lost the public dimension of their pain. It is, Ferrante explains, the deep-rooted mistake of every city to lay claim to be a city of love without labyrinths, to believe you can give birth to a future with no Furies lying in wait. The same blinkered, anaesthetised, radically disabling vision with which most official discourse in the modern world hounds its mothers.

Behind one half of Ferrante's pen name, Elena, is a tale from Greek mythology. According to a relatively little-known version of the story, Zeus rapes and impregnates, not Leda the swan, but Nemesis, who turns herself into a goose to escape him. She then lays an egg, found by a shepherd and handed to Leda, who nurtures it and out of which Elena is born, who is then raised by Leda, in Ferrante's suggestive formula, as 'her daughter-non-daughter'.[4] It must be one of the earliest stories of surrogacy, as well as offering a model of motherhood without vested interest because it has embraced a stranger. It can also be read as a veiled warning on the part of Ferrante to anyone trying to track her down, or claiming – as if that settled anything – to have done so. Behind the name she has chosen as an author lies a story of gestation that cannot be traced to a single source. It is through ancient gods, animal matter, humans that her writing is born, travelling across species and time. Repeatedly, Ferrante has said that she preserved her anonymity so that her books, free of the bluster and publicity of her presence, could make their way without her, like a child leaving home.

Instead, the modern cult of the author, not to speak of the constant pressure on Ferrante to identify herself, straps the literary work to the writer, as if the only possible link between a text and its creator is that of a domineering mother – about whom Ferrante has much to say – who cannot bear to let her children go: 'doesn't someone who reads one of my books make space in his own vocabulary for my words, doesn't he appropriate them, if necessary doesn't he reuse them?'[5] This is strikingly reminiscent of another central concept of D. W. Winnicott, the use of an object, which refers to the ruthlessness any infant must use in the struggle with and against the mother to survive.[6] In Ferrante's second novel, *The Days of Abandonment* (2002), Olga, abandoned wife and mother, reflects on the complications of her new life: 'In this reasoning, I seemed to capture all the absurdity of the adjective "my," "my children"'[7] (the same formula that had so appalled Colonel Pargiter's grandson in Woolf's novel *The Years*). It takes time, and she almost doesn't make it, but, bracingly and bit by bit, her agony at her loss beckons – for her, for her children – a kind of freedom.

We might also note in passing that for the journalist who, in an act of flagrant misogyny, claimed to have exposed Ferrante's true identity, her greatest offence was to have misrepresented her own mother (as Neapolitan dressmaker in the novel rather than Holocaust survivor in her real life). As if to say: mothers must not be reinvented. Fiction is fine so long as it does not trespass on – violate – the sacred domain of mothers. He probably didn't realise that, in his proud, vulgar gesture of exposure, he was close to imitating the brute husband of Ferrante's first novel, *Troubling Love* (1999), who more or less strips his wife bare as a gypsy in a series of paintings he brazenly peddles for profit (he then beats her at the first sign of a sexuality over which he has no control). 'How was it possible,' their daughter asks, 'that my father could hand over, to vulgar men, bold and seductive versions of that body which if necessary he would defend with murderous rage?'[8] In *Troubling Love*, such behaviour is not restricted to men alone. The daughter also goes crazy at any sign of her mother's independent sexual life, and indeed betrays her mother's love affair to her father.

In Ferrante's vision, the world conspires to conceal the bodies of mothers. Merely having one is a crime. 'No one, starting with the mother's dressmaker, must think that a mother has a woman's body' – Ferrante had wanted to make these lines by Elsa Morante, her favourite Italian woman writer, the epigraph to the novel.[9] We have seen this hatred of a mother's sexual being before: the flight from what Ferrante calls, in another memorable formula, 'the erotic vapor' of the mother's body.[10] The brazen exposure of Ferrante taps into this set of tired, ugly stereotypes born of possessiveness and rage. Why would anyone – a woman, a mother – hide herself unless she was guilty?

The name Elena will take up its central role as Elena Greco, the narrator of the Neapolitan Novels. But before that, Leda and Elena give their names, both sourced from the Greeks, to the main characters of Ferrante's third novel, *The Lost Daughter*, published in 2006, when she was already renowned in Italy but before the Quartet made her internationally famous. Leda is a middle-aged mother who finds herself caught up in a 'complicated, modern question of maternity', which leads her, and not for the first time, to leave her children. Making her escape from any remaining parental responsibilities for her two grown daughters, she heads off for a beach holiday on the Ionian coast, where she finds herself obsessively watching a little girl, Elena, as she plays with her young mother, and whose lost doll she finds and then keeps (without her doll the child sickens, and her mother, whom Leda has befriended, wishes brain cancer on whoever stole it).

The story inverts the original Leda–Elena myth. Instead of generously nurturing another's child, a mother finds herself enacting a form of cruelty towards

someone else's daughter, which she can no more prevent herself from doing, or bring to an end, than she
can explain it to herself.[11] As a young mother, she abandoned her own children for two years as the only way of
surviving, although her motives are not entirely clear to
her, and certainly to nobody else. Although the book has
received relatively little attention outside Italy, Ferrante
has described *The Lost Daughter* as her most risk-taking
novel and the one to which she is most painfully bound;
without the 'great anxiety' it cost her, she wouldn't have
written the first of the Neapolitan Novels, *My Brilliant
Friend*.[12] 'The most difficult things to tell,' she comments
on her anguished attachment to this novel, 'are those
which we ourselves can't understand' (these are Leda's
own words in the text).[13] 'What I wanted of [my chil-
dren],' Leda ponders, 'I never understood, I don't know
even now.'[14] This is a mother whose deepest clarity stems
from her lack of knowing, from her acceptance that to
be a mother is to relinquish control of the human heart.

Ferrante is issuing another warning, this time against
the idea that motherhood is a locked closet to which
the best literary writing on the topic would offer the
one true key – again rather like a mother who allows
her child no secrets or lies, and claims fully to know her
child's mind. On the folly of such an idea, *The Days of
Abandonment* already offered a hint, in the deranging
episode when Olga struggles frantically with her daughter, Ilaria, to lock and unlock their front door (the only

moment of sanity occurs when the mother admits to herself and her daughter that the whole thing makes no sense). In Ferrante's writing, you do not solve the problem or question of motherhood. You enter, at whatever risk, into its space. 'The literary truth of motherhood,' she observes, 'is yet to be explored.' 'The task of the woman writer today,' is not to 'keep talking about it in an idyllic way,' as they do in the guidebooks, which leaves mothers feeling 'alone and guilty,' but 'to delve truthfully into the darkest depth.'[15] A recent study suggests that the mothers who read the most manuals on mothering report the highest level of depressive symptoms (it is not clear whether the depression is the consequence of reading so many manuals or the reason they are reading them in the first place).[16]

Elena Ferrante's literary portrayal of motherhood takes you about as far from manuals and guidebooks as you could possibly hope to get. It is like nothing else I have read, which is why in this book Ferrante is the author with a chapter to herself. The Swedish publisher Bromberg, who acquired the rights to *The Days of Abandonment* and had the work translated, decided against publication on the grounds that the mother's behaviour was 'morally reprehensible'.[17] One can only wonder what they thought of what came later, since in Ferrante's world, mothers regularly walk out on their children; neglect or forget about them in favour of writing and/or sexual passion; love and hate, protect and resent, guide and thwart them in equal measure. At times, children seem to be no more than pawns in the adult sexual game – in the final volume of the Neapolitan Novels, a mother picks up her friend's baby daughter to flirt with the father who was once her own lover, ignoring her own daughter, who, in a blink of an eye, disappears for ever. (Echoing the title of Ferrante's third novel, *The Lost Daughter*, the last in the Quartet has the title *The Story of the Lost Child*).

'The risk that Leda runs,' Ferrante comments, cutting straight to the heart of the dilemma faced by so many modern mothers, 'seems to me all in that question: can I, a woman of today, succeed in being loved by my daughters, in loving them, without having of necessity to sacrifice myself and therefore hate myself?'[18] Mothers, especially mothers and daughters, are everywhere, although often overlooked by reviewers of her work. On this matter, Ferrante herself is clear. 'Sometimes,' she comments on the mother–daughter relationship, 'I think I haven't written about anything else.'[19] Motherhood is the irreducible core of her fiction. And not just at the level of theme, since it trails the very act of writing mercilessly in its wake: 'To write truly,' Olga instructs herself in *The Days of Abandonment* as she tries to pick up her own neglected fiction, 'is to speak from the depths of the maternal womb.'[20]

*

In the Neapolitan Novels, Elena Greco, who goes by the name of Lenù, is part of a dyad, the other half of which is Raffaella Cerullo (called Lila by Lenù, and Lina by everyone else). One can only assume that this confusing proximity of their names is intentional, a way of registering the often suffocating intimacy that binds them, the oscillation of the two women as they repeatedly attempt to move apart – even to reject each other – and then, with no less virulence and passion, come back together again (the Quartet has been greeted as the first in-depth literary rendering of friendship between women). The novels are written in Lenù's voice, but even that is not obvious. Lenù takes her inspiration from a piece of writing by Lila from their childhood, when they were planning a glorious future together as writers, a future that would make them rich and famous. The Quartet ends with Lenù discovering reams of writing by Lila on the architectural and cultural history of Naples, to which she has been devoting herself as she grieves the never-explained disappearance of her youngest child several years before.

At one point, they do indeed compose a piece of journalistic writing together, when they decide to expose the violence of the men who have done their worst to control and destroy the two women's lives and the lives of all those around them in their small, desperately inverted community in Naples. Although it is Lenù who fulfils their childhood dream by becoming a famous writer, she is for ever haunted by the feeling that it is Lila who is the true author of her work. Ferrante has said that the two women are minted from the same coin. But by placing uncertain authorship right at the heart of these novels, Ferrante is doing more than reflecting her own nuanced, fractured position as a writer. She has also opened up a space, agonising or liberating dependent on your point of view, where a woman can at least ask herself, with reference to the moment deemed by general consent to be her moment of most glorious creativity: to whom or what exactly is a woman giving birth?

It is often said that having a baby reintroduces a woman to her own mother (in its most gloating version, this is assumed to be because the experience is so difficult that she at last understands and forgives her mother everything). In another account, when a first baby turns out to be the spitting image of the father, with features bearing no trace of the mother, she will be consoled that this is nature's way of making the father feel secure that his progeny is his own, a fact of which no father can be easily certain. Along similar lines, the French avant-garde film-maker Jean-Luc Godard wryly observed, with reference to his 1985 film *Je vous salue, Marie* or *Hail Mary*, that Joseph's dilemma when faced with Mary's pregnancy and her claim to have been visited by God – a likely story, as one might say – was simply the dilemma of all men confronted with the prospect of fatherhood. French law states: 'the child of a married woman will be presumed to be the child of the husband' (thereby recognising that no one really has the faintest idea).[21]

The paternity of Lila's first child, Rino (named after her brother), is initially attributed to her lover, then finally and reluctantly to her former husband, to the distress of the two men who might have fathered him. But Ferrante also lets us inside this quandary from the other side, giving the Greek vision of the mother as passive receptacle of the male seed a Gothic, feminist twist. Men 'show up inside us and withdraw', Lenù muses, 'leaving, concealed in our flesh, their ghost, like a lost object'.[22] She is contemplating the various offspring of Nino, whom she first loved in childhood, one of the possible fathers of Lila's child, and by whom she too will become pregnant (he has had at least one other child along the way and will have two more by the woman he eventually marries). As so often, Lila is characteristically more blunt: 'Men insert their thingy inside you and you become a box of flesh with a living doll inside.'[23]

Dolls are central. The Quartet begins with Lila and Lenù hurling their cherished dolls into the basement of the house of the dreaded Don Achille Caracci, characterised in the cast list provided for each volume as 'the ogre of fairy tales'. It ends with the two dolls magically reappearing in a parcel received by Lenù, one assumes posted by Lila, who has disappeared (Tina, the name of Lenù's doll, is also the name of Lila's lost child). This in itself can be read as another caution. Ferrante's dolls live on another planet from the maternal instinct they are most commonly assumed to personify. On this, Ferrante finds herself in harmony with Freud, who was criticised for daring to suggest that a little girl playing with her doll, far from anticipating some maternal idyll, was engaged in an act of mastery as she exerted on the hapless creature the control she suffered at the hands of her mother. 'A mother is only a daughter who plays,' Leda thinks to herself as she enacts various hideous rituals on the doll she has stolen. 'I was playing now.'[24]

The first pregnancy in the Neapolitan Novels is that of Pinuccia, who marries Lila's brother Rino, and who turns against her own baby the moment he is born: 'He's ugly, he's uglier than Rino, that whole family is ugly'; 'It's my fault, I made a bad choice of a husband, but when you're a girl, you don't think about it, and now look at what a child I've had.'[25] Lenù had gone to visit her, thinking she would find her 'in bed, happy, with the baby at her breast'.[26] In Naples, girls, like Pinuccia and also Lila, are married as young as sixteen. Ferrante passes no judgement – on this she is scrupulous. Pinuccia is not an inadequate mother. It is the world around her that has failed.

In Ferrante's writing, it is a cruel society that is indicted on behalf of mothers. Pinuccia's rage – again like Lila, who does everything to thwart pregnancy in the first years of a wretched marriage – spreads from a brutal male-dominated community that stifles its women and girls in their hearts and the deepest recesses of their bodies: 'I looked at her stomach,' Lenù ponders about Lila when her failure to become pregnant is making her husband's masculinity a joke, 'and imagined that truly inside it, every day, every night, she was fighting a battle to destroy the life that Stefano wanted to insert there by force.'[27] The community is less charitable – like a Greek chorus, it spreads the rumour that Lila is suffocating the foetus in her womb. The old belief that women smothered their unborn child is thus neatly cast by Ferrante, either as an act of desperate agency and defiance on behalf of oppressed women, or as the vicious assault on mothers it always was.

In Ferrante's world, it is not only men who invade the bodies and souls of women. Like Sylvia Plath before her, she has the ability – on the same page or in what can feel like a hair's breadth from each other – to indict patriarchy and ask what, in the daughter's relation to her mother, women might be no less up against ('Sometimes I think I haven't written about anything else'). For once you ask the question of who or what is germinating, taking up residence inside the body of the mother – whether in a gesture of openness or dread – then there is no telling, at least not for any of Ferrante's women, what you might find. She thus takes the idea of the stranger inside the mother a further, disconcerting step. A mother's body is a crowded space, like the community of Naples, where everybody is jostling, impinging on and invading everybody else.

As Leda watches Elena on the beach she sees the extended family close in on the little girl, like all the relations from whom she as a young woman had, or thought she had, fled: 'I had them all inside me.'[28] She feels revulsion at the 'ancestors compressed into the child's flesh', and anger when mother and child project their fake-adult and fake-child voices into the doll as if it were speaking with one and the same voice.[29] In flight from such cloying osmosis and from her unwelcome inner guests, Leda had dreamed of her pregnancy as a brave new world: 'I was not my grandmother (seven children), I was not my mother (four daughters), I was not my aunts, my cousins.'[30] One of Lenù's strongest desires is to escape her mother, whose bitter, limping frame trails across all four books: 'I have to eliminate her.'[31]

Such control is of course an illusion. You can leave, grow away from, forge your own path, but you cannot eliminate the tie to the mother. From the relative safety of Milan, where she has escaped as a young student, Lenù trembles at the thought of her potential future as a mother: 'And if my mother should emerge from my stomach just now when I think I am safe?'[32] Like a contrary, or even perverse, fairy godmother – I mean that as the greatest compliment – Ferrante grants the mothers of her fiction the strongest impulse to freedom and closes in on that very impulse more or less in the same breath. After her third pregnancy Lenù starts limping. Like all daughters, she has been gifted by her mother in all the painful ambiguity of the term. On her deathbed, when they are partly reconciled, her mother confesses to her that, for all her tirades against her, she was her favourite – in some ways her one and only – child, a fact to which those very tirades bore witness, while also expressing her resentment that her daughter has left her to make another world and name for herself. 'The only good thing in her life,' Lenù reports their conversation, 'was the moment I came out of her belly, I, her first child.'[33] To that day, her mother had experienced all her other children as a punishment (a feeling she saw as her greatest sin). The reconciliation is a mixed blessing: 'When she embraced me before I left, it was as if she meant to slip inside me and stay there, as once I had been inside her.'[34] Lenù tells Lila that she has started limping as a way of keeping her mother alive.

Ferrante's writing begins here, following in the paths of writers like Sylvia Plath and Edith Wharton, or in tune with Ariel Leve, on the perils of a mother's proximity to her child. Or at least her first published writing begins here, since by her own account, until *Troubling Love* she 'abandoned' many stories, as if her own career, like her novels, were littered with the debris of children lost or discarded along the way. In *Troubling Love*, the dead mother, Amalia, who committed suicide, steadily invades her daughter Delia, 'like a hot liquid that had been injected into me at some unknown time'.[35] Like Lenù, she 'had wanted to eliminate every root I had in her, even the deepest', especially – like a deranged lover – every inch of her mother that she could not know, control or even reach. She fails. Slowly she recrafts herself in her mother's image, down to the smallest gesture and item of her clothing, until finally she takes down Amalia's suitcase, the one she was carrying the night she died, and puts on her clothes: 'I felt that the old garment was the final narrative that my mother had left me, and that now, with all the necessary adjustments, it fit me like a glove.' Then she adjusts her hair – a curl over the right eye, two broad bands meeting in a wave over her forehead – to 'that old-fashioned hairstyle, popular in the forties but already rare at the end of the fifties': '[It] suited me. Amalia had been. I was Amalia' (the last lines of the book).[36] The intense focus of these short early novels will not be repeated. Unfettered by the *longue durée* of the Neapolitan Quartet still to come, they each take a single acute moment of crisis in the life of a mother and/or daughter and stretch it to breaking point.

In Ferrante's vision, 'troubling love' *is*, therefore, the love between mother and daughter, the template for every subsequent emotional attachment, for the agony and ecstasy of a life, for every love affair. Which means that whatever the trials and traumas and pleasures of women's relationships with men, they can only be its pale shadow. Freud suggested that all eros starts at the mother's breast and, even more tellingly, that a woman always – at least first time round – marries a man who is the stand-in for the lost mother (a student once came to see me, disturbed by the implication of this insight that, deep inside the heart, only mothers were therefore to be found). Note, too, the ambiguity of Ferrante's titles – *The Lost Daughter, The Story of the Lost Child* – which can be parsed from the viewpoint either of the daughter or the mother: a child feeling lost in the world (perhaps redeemable), a child who vanishes without trace.

Ferrante has stated that she is at once drawn to and ambivalent about psychoanalysis – she calls it the 'lexicon of the precipice' – and about Freud, but on this much she is happy to give him credit. Every love relationship, good or bad, she explains, is a reactivation of this primitive bond; for women, no marriage can expel that first troubling love 'the *only* love-conflict that in every case lasts forever'; Olga in *The Days of Abandonment* was only ever faithful to the husband before he left her because he became for her 'the cocoon of fantasies tied to the mother' (which is why the abandonment is so devastating).[37] As I read interviews with Ferrante, it seems to me that she is more assertive about this – or to put it another way, more confident in her terror at this mother–daughter reality – than about almost anything else.

*

If the story of mothers stopped there it would already be troubling enough. But Ferrante's portrayal of these mothers takes another pivotal step. The mother–daughter relationship, the pregnancy that contains the mother and all her forebears – 'And if my mother should emerge from my stomach just now when I think I am safe?' – is where the world loses its bearings and all boundaries dissolve (giving the lie to the idea that any mother can hold everything in place). As we have touched on in earlier chapters, allowing borders to open, recognising the radical fragility of the boundaries we create, can also be seen, in relation to mothers, as the foundation for a different ethics and, perhaps, a different world. For me, Ferrante is the writer who pushes this possibility as far as it can go, notably in a world in which the myth of self-containment and self-control is being promoted harder than ever.

To this myth, motherhood in its most troubling guise can be understood as a kind of angry, exasperated riposte. It has always struck me that what needs explaining is, not the moments where our most cherished individuality fails, but the extraordinary fact that, emerging from the first morass of being, we ever buy into the illusion that we are self-sufficient, radically distinguishable individuals to begin with: our bodies our property, our minds subordinate to our will, the whole world – this is the most dangerous version – at our command. Ferrante is having none of it. The story begins, she states, 'when, one after another, our borders collapse'.[38] 'Borders make us feel stable' – she is making a feminist point:

At the first hint of conflict, at the least threat, we close them ... The history of women in the past hundred years is based on the very dangerous 'crossing of the boundary' imposed by patriarchal cultures. The results have been extraordinary in all fields. But the force with which they want to carry us back inside the old borders is no less extraordinary. It is manifested as pure crude, bloody violence.[39]

Lila's husband beats her, and on at least one occasion rapes her in front of their child. Women like her and Amalia who 'refuse to be subjugated' find themselves up against the ultimatum: '"Either you'll be the way I say or I'll change you by beating you till I kill you."'[40] To this all too familiar ultimatum for women, Ferrante adds her own unique dimension. The battle of the sexes does not just pit one will and force against another – although it surely does that too. Rather, a woman who refuses to respect the existing boundaries of a patri-archal world evokes a whole other, terrifying psychic space. Shattering the carapace of selfhood, she brings to the surface the physical and mental fragments, the bits and pieces that, at the deepest level, we truly are, though we mostly resist such knowledge with all our might. 'What corrupts us,' she observes, 'is the passion for ourselves, the urgent need for our own primacy.'[41] Such proud, corrupt self-affirmation is not something that she herself has escaped: 'It's blindingly obvious that

I alone authorized myself . . . What is this if not pride?'[42]

Ferrante's writing career to date might be read as a plea for us to reconsider: we truly would be better off starting – recognising that as humans of 'woman born' we all start – from somewhere quite else. 'It seemed to me,' she states, 'that feeling literally in pieces could be traced back to that sort of original fragmentation that is bringing into the world-coming into the world.'[43] She knows she is walking on the wild side: 'I remain convinced that it's also essential to describe the dark side of the pregnant body, which is omitted in order to bring out the luminous side, the Mother of God.'[44] Divine perfection, moral purity is not what she is talking about. Rather, the pregnant body brings us close to the animal component of our nature, frightening in so far as it reminds us 'of the instability of the forms assumed by life'.[45] The task is to recognise this, rather than aiming for some transcendence, or even hatred, of pregnancy into a refined world of rules and etiquette, as if leaving the swamp of pregnancy behind – we have been here before – were the world's only saving grace.

Ferrante's mothers are not themselves innocent of the impulse to salvage pregnancy from itself (they are not innocent of anything). They are, after all, in it up to their necks. When she was expecting her second child, Leda tells us, she was distraught at the prospect of 'giving up of any sublimation of my pregnancy': 'My body became a bloody liquid; suspended in it was a mushy

sediment which grew a violent polyp, so far from anything human that it reduced me, even though it fed and
grew, to rotting matter without life'; whereas her first
baby was right away 'a being at its best, purified of
humours and blood, humanized, intellectualized, with
nothing that could evoke the blind cruelty of living matter as it expands'.[46] I have never come across writing on
the topic of pregnancy quite like this.

Needless to say, and as any mother who has given
birth will tell you, the baby most often turns out to be
the exact opposite in character from what the experience of pregnancy might lead a mother to expect, as if
to remind the mother that her body, finally, is – but also
is not – what it is all about. Furthermore, the experience
of pregnancy is rarely a reliable guide to how a woman
will mother her baby. Lenù's pregnancies are a source
of expansiveness and joy, Lila's mainly of displeasure
bordering on horror. When Lenù tries to reassure her,
she reproaches her that she has simply learned to use
the 'sentimental voice of our mothers'.[47] 'She seemed
ready,' Lenù writes when they later find themselves pregnant together, 'to find any joy I found in motherhood
a betrayal.'[48] And yet, it is Lila who, after the birth of
her son, turns out to be the 'best mother in the whole
neighbourhood'.[49] Pinuccia brings her baby to her to
look after, in the hope that her gifts as a mother will
benefit her son. Whereas, as soon as they get home from
the hospital, Lenù's first baby sucks for a few moments,

then 'shrieks like a furious little animal', and writhes and screams for hours: 'What was wrong with me? What poison had polluted my milk?'[50]

Anyone looking for a counter-narrative on the joys of breastfeeding could do worse than read Ferrante, where they will also find another of those rare testimonies to its scandalous, incestuous sensuality (the erotic pleasure and the pain, two intensities mostly absent from the conventional narrative, are again surely linked). Here, too, Ferrante is pushing the boat out. In a letter to the editors of the Italian literary magazine *L'Indice*, she describes a childhood memory of her and her sister watching their mother feeding a new arrival, until, once the baby unwillingly slid into sleep, 'our mother smiled at us with her dark eyes and let white drops from her breasts drip into our mouths, a warm, sweet taste that stunned us.'[51] This long letter at the heart of her collection, *Frantumaglia*, is one of the rare occasions where Ferrante states that she is responding to her interlocutors' questions with pleasure.[52]

During her first pregnancy, Lila's greatest fear was that the thing she most dreaded would happen and that she would break apart, overflow. Remember Sylvia Plath: 'I am breaking apart like the world' (likewise Ferrante: 'I know what it means to break apart').[53] They are not alone. Compare Lucy Jones writing today against the guidebook vision of pregnancy as 'pastel-hued dream': 'surely I am dying or at least splitting in half. Cut her out, cut her out, cut her out. I am birthing a hurricane. A spiked mace. A heap of barbed wire. A bladed melon. An inflated pufferfish.'[54] But Ferrante gives to this experience an additional twist. It is through Lila's very fear – her being so much more in touch with blind matter and the fragmentation of the world – that she finds herself capable of loving 'that absurd modality of life, that expanding module' inside her.[55] Stuffed inside the stolen doll of *The Lost Daughter*, Leda finds a worm put there by Elena to pretend to make it pregnant. 'I have a horror of crawling things,' she observes, 'but for that clot of humours I felt a naked pity.'[56] She is, literally, scraping the depths.

And yet out of such matter Ferrante re-creates the seeds of ethical life. 'I would like to narrate in a meaningful way how a woman approaches, through the requirements of caring for someone, through love, the repulsiveness of the flesh, those areas where the mediation of the world becomes weak.'[57] Repulsiveness of the flesh, the world's mediations faltering – this is not how love, or motherhood, are normally thought about. We are light years from the terms mostly used to prescribe, purify, sanitise the task of mothering. We might also be getting closer to understanding the dangers faced by a mother, by anyone, when they welcome a stranger in their midst. Which is perhaps why alien mothers landing on our shores to give birth find themselves the objects of such visceral revulsion.

*

To explain what her own mother bequeathed to her, Ferrante offers the word *frantumaglia* – in fact, the term, all hints and murmurs and overheard sounds, explains nothing. The word gives the title to the collection of essays and interviews, all conducted by correspondence, from which many of the statements by Ferrante cited so far in this chapter have been taken. It is a book that, among other things, serves as a sustained rejoinder to the resentments provoked by her refusal to release her true name and take proper charge of her writing: she has everything to say about her writing, and about what her characters and novels mean to her, but not one thing about how anyone should read her books. But it also seems to me as if Ferrante, in interview after interview, as energised as she often appears reluctant, is 'dream-reading' her own work – the term she uses to describe how a true literary work takes off from its author to engender something new and unanticipated in the reader (which makes the unconscious the slipstream of all new birth).[58]

This is where a mother's disintegration, loss of self, falling into pieces, so central to Ferrante's writing, begins. *Frantumaglia* is a word of dialect that her mother used when she was 'racked by contradictory sensations that were tearing her apart', which depressed her, made her dizzy and her mouth taste like iron.[59] The word for an unfathomable disquiet, it referred to 'a miscellaneous crowd of things in her head, debris in a muddy water of the brain', the source of all suffering 'not traceable to a single obvious cause'.[60] The strongest memory it evokes is of her mother weeping '*frantumaglia* tears'.[61] *Frantumaglia* arrived as a warning that her mother was losing herself – it would drive her suddenly out of the house, leaving a pot burning on the stove. This memory of her mother in pain is the seedbed of Ferrante's writing: Olga, distracted, walking out of the house; the copper pot that explodes in *My Brilliant Friend*, the first warning shot that Lila is cursed with a gift that shatters the world's contours.[62]

But vivid and poignant as this memory appears, it is also a complete mystery: to the mother herself, and then to Ferrante, the daughter who cannot now ask her mother what on earth the word meant, and who for that reason – obedient to a legacy as generative as it is scary – has no choice but to make the word her own. What mothers pass to daughters, Ferrante is also telling us, is language, not as a tool but in the form of words that endlessly slide from our grasp. It is this fundamental recalcitrance of language, its inner resistance to the meanings it is meant to promote – like the sexuality no mother can herself fully know or own – that led Jean Laplanche to argue that all mothers are an eternal enigma to their child, presenting the child with an insoluble sexual riddle that will spur their curiosity for life.

When Ferrante picks up the term *frantumaglia*, its meanings quiver and darken, and this in turn will be the legacy she passes to Lila – her best-loved character, as she acknowledges, because she forced her to work so hard.[63] 'The *frantumaglia* is an unstable landscape, an infinite aerial or aquatic mass of debris that appears to the I, brutally, as its true and unique inner self.'[64] She is on her own home ground: 'I who sometimes suffer the illness of Olga,' she comments, 'represent it [*frantumaglia*] mainly to myself as a hum growing louder and a vortex-like fracturing of material living and dead: a swarm of bees approaching above the motionless tree-tops; the sudden eddy in a slow body of water.'[65] As we have already seen, this thrum of being that Ferrante sources in the body of the mother, however agonised, is the precondition of creativity. *Frantumaglia* evokes a moment of childhood, before language instilled speech, a 'bright-coloured explosion of sounds, thousands and thousands of butterflies with sonorous wings'.[66] For the mother, *frantumaglia* was the bad spirit of the household, its spilled remnants gently bruising the fragile discipline of the home. As a daughter and as a writer, Ferrante has added colour and sound, rendering her mother's anguish cosmic.

That rare moment of identification with her character Olga and her illness – 'I who sometimes suffer the illness of Olga' – should give us pause, since if there is one easy way out of all this mess, it would be to label Ferrante's own suffering mother, together with Lila and all the rest of these mothers, as sick. This is a charge I have heard levelled at mothers merely for falling in love with a man other than their husband, or at the first hint of discontent – another common ploy being to attribute all maternal unhappiness to the onset of the menopause (one mother who had tried to leave the father of her children told me that, in the course of her marriage, he had diagnosed her at least four times as suffering from the menopause, which defies the laws of biology, if nothing else).

Lila's moments of 'dissolving margins', as she describes them, reach the limits of what is bearable, for herself and for Lenù, who, it would be fair to say, is the person who loves her most. They turn the world dark, as if an intense black mass of a storm were scudding across the night sky, reducing the moon to insensate matter; or, in the midst of an earthquake, dissolving the boundaries of the driver of the car and the car itself, in which she is sitting: 'the thing and the person gushing out of themselves, mixing liquid metal and flesh'.[67] Lenù struggles against this vision but she also, on occasion, imbibes it: 'I thought: yes, Lila is right, the beauty of things is a trick, the sky is a throne of fear . . . I am part of the universal terror; at this moment I'm the infinitesimal particle through which the fear of everything becomes conscious.'[68] As she sits on the beach, she finds herself hoping that mad dogs, vipers, scorpions, enormous sea serpents and assassins will emerge from the sea to torture her.[69] This is frightening, but unlike forms of mental disturbance that lock the sufferer inside her own head, it is shared, passing back and forth between the two friends. And, as we will shortly see, Lila's unique insight, which she is calling up on behalf of everyone, can be understood as drawing out the dark substance of the earth, together with its political terrors.

There is, therefore, a way of reading the Neapolitan Novels that would see Lenù not just as Lila's best friend (the two being parts of each other's innermost being) but also as a mother who feels her only task in life is to contain – to ward off – the nightmares of her child: 'I who have written for months and months,' she writes at the end of the final volume, sweeping the entire work up in such a protective impulse, 'to give her a form whose boundaries won't dissolve, and defeat her, and calm her, and so in turn calm myself.'[70] They are the last lines of the Quartet (followed only by the epilogue). This would make the entire Quartet an act of mothering, albeit with a difference, since in this version the only way of soothing the world is first to call up its worst demons. I remember one of the people dearest to me in the world asking me about my baby daughter: 'How will you help her with her fear?' (which at least has the virtue of seeing that there can be no allaying a child's fear – nor indeed anybody else's – unless you acknowledge the fear in the first place). Lenù also knows that without that fear she would surely not be able to write: 'Would I know how to imagine those things without her? Would I know how to give life to every object, let it bend in unison with mine?'[71] This, finally, is the genius of Lila – my *brilliant* friend.

Ferrante is by no means the only writer, nor indeed the first, to make this link between mothering and the contours of the universe. To take just one striking instance, in this case rendered from the point of view of a son: William Maxwell's 1937 novel *They Came Like Swallows* is a vivid portrait of a mother, Elizabeth, who will leave two young boys when she dies of Spanish flu in the pandemic of 1918. In the mind of her eight-year-old Bunny, all lines converge on her body. She must be present to secure his domestic space: 'all the lines and surfaces of the room bend toward his mother, so that when he looked at the pattern of the rug, he saw it necessarily in relation to the toe of her shoe.'[72] Only then can he allow his possessions to be at times 'what they actually were' and at others to become 'knights and crusaders, or airplanes or elephants in a procession'.[73] Unless the world is kept in its shape by the mother, there can be no imaginative freedom. Unless there is a mother, there can be no world. But the same mother also threatens the very contours she holds in place. When she kisses Bunny, 'everything blurred'; when he lies in bed not quite awake listening to her conversation with his aunt Irene, 'the white woodwork was unattached to the walls, the shape of chairs was ambiguous . . . while he squinted his eyes, the walls relaxed and became shapeless.'[74] Ferrante gives a modern-day version of this inherent instability of all forms, which Lila raises to the nth dimension.

*

As we saw earlier, one of the plaints and limitations of the modern mother in the West today is that she so often finds herself adrift from the wider world, from public, political life. To that extent, the idea of the 'working mother' is to my mind one of the misnomers of all time, since the one thing such a mother must never think of doing is taking her baby or children to work. If Medea and Dido are heroines for Ferrante, it is at least partly because of the way their anger spreads outwards from their personal despair, bringing down whole dynasties and cities in its wake – whereas today, as Ferrante puts it, women can enter the city provided they do not try to reinvent it.[75] Such women are connected and powerful, however tragically things turn out in the end. In their eyes, their most intimate rejection is an injustice, one that the whole world needs to hear about.

If Ferrante is so resonant for the argument of this book, it is not only because of the way she ploughs the darkest depths of the maternal psyche, excavating, as terror and vision, the aspects of being human that are hardest for anyone to contemplate. Nor is it just that, in her literary hands, pregnancy becomes the original dissolution of all form, in which the world, if it would only shed its most oppressive, self-centred delusions, would do well to recognise itself. It is also because of the way – in one last, perhaps unexpected, twist – she folds this vision into the political reality out of which it at least partly grows, and on which it so violently propagates and feeds itself.

In Ferrante's vision, a mother's body and the public world all around her are indissolubly linked – her rejoinder to the idea we have repeatedly come across that these two opposite realms of being a mother, at their most intense, are best sidelined or not spoken about. The community of Naples in which Lila and Lenù live is drenched in a violence that stems from a resurgent post-war Italian fascism. This violence pervades the meat factory where Lila works under inhuman conditions, a war zone between communists and fascists where her boss is finally murdered; the proud and struggling business enterprises of the community steeped in dirty money, bribery and corruption; the assaults, mental and physical, on women; the safety, or rather non-safety, of the streets from where children are seized without warning or redress. It is not just mothers who grow, unwelcome, inside their daughters' pregnant bodies. It is a whole vicious political dispensation that is threatening to be reborn. The fear lived out by Lenù on the beach is, therefore, also a political fear that passes indiscriminately from body to body, hand to mouth. These women, these mothers, are alert to it like nobody else.

The agonies of the mothering body – to give the term 'labour pains' an added gloss – are at one with the drag and flow of the community in which they take place. 'Lila and Elena [Lenù] are made of the neighbourhood's matter,' Ferrante comments, 'but a fluid matter that drags everything along in its wake.'[76]

In this context, to be a mother is to struggle to save – while also knowing that you will fail to save – your child. To be faced with the prospect that the world is not getting better, that there will not be a better life for the lives you have made (a feeling that for so many in the world as I write is becoming more intense by the day). Violence breeds violence. In order to save herself and her son, Lila thinks, she 'had to intimidate those who wished to intimidate her, she had to inspire fear in those who wished to make her fear'.[77] At times, writing is contaminated by the same vision. 'One writes not so much to write,' Lenù muses in the midst of the struggle against the Solara brothers, 'one writes to inflict pain on those who wish to inflict pain.'[78] Get in there first (another, deadly, type of cross-border exchange). Children are not spared. In one of the grimmest moments in the Quartet, Silvia, a political activist, arrives at Lila's home having been beaten and raped by fascists, and tells her story 'as if she were recounting a horrendous nursery rhyme'.[79] Lenù's daughter Elsa is in the room. When Lenù goes to find her other daughter, Dede, she finds her playing with Silvia's son Mirko (another child of Nino's). She is instructing him: '*You have to hit me, understand?*'[80] 'The new living flesh was replicating the old in a game.'[81]

What is a mother meant to do in such a world? Might it be kinder to mothers to lift from their minds and bodies the impossible expectation that they can repair the world and make it safe? And if the world took on its own responsibilities for the mess that it makes? 'We *are*,' Ferrante states, 'the destabilising conditions we suffer or cause.'[82] Naples is 'a male city ungovernable in both its public and private behaviour',[83] but it took time for her to realise that her flight from Naples, which was above all a flight from its mothers, was futile, that what she needed to recognise was the 'torture of women, to feel the weight of the male city on their existence'.[84] This makes the flight from the mother a form of political blindness. Or rather, it makes the mother answerable, the scapegoat for a political distress of which no mother could possibly be the single source, but for which she inevitably will be blamed. At moments in the Quartet, it is as if every dissolution of form flows indiscriminately from the violent politics of the city streets. In vocabulary strikingly evocative of the miasma that bears down on Lila, Ferrante describes the city as 'a dark force of the world that weighs on its subjects, the sum total of what we call the threatening reality of today, engulfing, through violence, every space of mediation and civil relationship around and within the characters'.[85] Lila can see into the violent heart of things, but none of it, not as wife or mother or daughter, is her fault.

'What do you think of the governing political class today?' one interviewer asks. 'I am repulsed by it,' Ferrante replies.[86] Later she elaborates: 'narratives that can state more directly, even through literature, the reasons for our repugnance as citizens are necessary.'[87] Note that she speaks as a citizen, which all mothers of course are, even if in modern times it does not always feel that way. But to be a citizen fully, you have to know you belong to the widest sweep of historical events. Ferrante's vision is expansive. The horror, the repugnance, cannot be restricted to – hived off onto – Naples, a metropolis that 'has anticipated and anticipates the troubles of Italy, perhaps of Europe'.[88] Slowly Lenù understands that Naples was part of a chain: 'with larger and larger links: the neighbourhood was connected to the city, the city to Italy, Italy to Europe, Europe to the whole planet'.[89] In which case, Lila's moments of breakdown cannot be hers alone. Rather, it is the rotting future of Europe and the whole universe that she is registering on behalf of everyone. In this, she is reminiscent of Freud's hysterics, whose symptoms allow the rest of the family to carry on behaving as if they, unlike the hysteric, are just fine. This makes Lila, not sick, but – to return once more to the Greeks – a prophetess. Or perhaps both: sick at heart and freighted with the cares of the world (the second being a common enough definition of motherhood).

*

In the course of working on this book, I have come to think that it is because this is the reality lying in wait once you scrape the surface of being a mother, a reality captured by Ferrante with such unforgiving intensity, that much public discourse on motherhood, tacking at top speed in the opposite direction, tends to be so glib, falsely knowing, cruel or anodyne. On the basis of conversations with my women friends who are mothers and devoted Ferrante fans, it would seem that her lack of inhibition on the subject of mothers plays a decisive part in her extraordinary success, making her readership – among which women do seem to predominate – something like a club or secret society, whose members have taken a vow never to explain exactly why they have joined or what, behind closed doors, they really talk about. When the boundaries of her characters dissolve, Ferrante observes of her own writing, 'the language with which they are attempting to say something about themselves also is loosened, unbounded.'[90] She has loosened the tongue and lifted a burden of guilt (we are far from Bettelheim). After all, what matters in the end is what can, and cannot, be said – an issue with added political urgency in our newly censored times. 'The most effective stories,' she states, 'are those that resemble ramparts from which one can gaze out at everything that has been excluded.'[91] Her simile – ramparts – is telling. Like de Beauvoir on the radical disorientation of mothering, she could be talking about the aliens on our shores.

Perhaps, then, it is not surprising that Ferrante's experience of writing should sail so close to her subject matter: 'In the Neapolitan Quartet, I wanted everything to take shape and then lose its shape.'[92] At first she needs tense, clear formulas that are 'demonstrations of beautiful form', but only as a pathway to writing that is 'disjointed, agitated, increasing the risk of absolute collapse' (when the borders collapse, 'the story begins').[93] She dreads the moment 'when the narrative has to compose itself again'.[94] She writes hundreds of pages without stopping, sometimes never needing to alter a single word, but she still prefers the rough draft to the finished product, 'writing that is dissatisfied with itself'.[95] Letting go of 'wriggling material' is, she states, 'the worst sin the writer can commit'.[96] Like the pregnant body, like Lila's mind, like the city – in harmony, or rather disharmony, with each other – writing expands, secretes, spills, dissolves, disintegrates. It is, remember, the boundaries that are fake: 'When we tell a story, the only thing that should matter is to find a cascade of our words that will flood all the marked-out territory with the persistence – even if devastating – of mucilage.'[97] This is writing as raw, viscous matter, like the worm that Leda found stuffed deep inside Elena's doll to make her pregnant. Remember Olga in *The Days of Abandonment*: 'To write truly is to speak from the depths of the maternal womb.'[98]

This chapter has the title 'The agony and the ecstasy'. I realise it may seem that the first of these has had the strongest voice. True, the broken edges of Ferrante's mothers and her writing are mostly in tune with the world's grief. But ecstasy is part of the picture. Over the years, Ferrante has come closer and closer to the idea that writing emerges out of an 'ecstatic condition': 'The ecstasy of the writing is feeling not the breath of the word that is liberated from the flesh but the flesh that has become one with the breath of the words.'[99] She calls it a 'disembodiment', but not, surely, as normally understood, since in this formula, flesh, far from being transcended, is now breathing through the words. What I hear her describing is a form of writing that lifts off only because it has immersed itself in the depths, beginning – as tends to be the case – with mothers: 'the literary truth [of motherhood] has yet to be explored . . . the task of a woman writer today is . . . to delve truthfully into the darkest depth.'[100] Or, to put it more simply, Elena Ferrante has let the cat out of the bag on behalf of mothers, and I, for one, could not be more grateful.

INSIDE OUT

To be a mother is to be saturated with the good and evil of the day. But unless you are very lucky, or privileged, or both, there is always the chance that evil will seize the hour, as my mother often tells me in relation to her never-ending grief for her daughter, my sister, who died more than twenty years ago. At the very least, it seems fair to say that, as much as a new, unpredictable beginning against the crush of totalitarian logic (Hannah Arendt's cry), each birth arrives with a history not of its own choosing. And since, to risk a cliché, there must surely be dark as well as lightness ahead, a mother who yearns most powerfully for her child to embody the free, the new, the best – as mothers mostly cannot help but do – is in danger of inscribing her denial of history, her own flight from suffering, across the body and mind of her child.

'Your nakedness,' Sylvia Plath addresses her newborn daughter in 'Morning Song', 'Shadows our safety.'[1] 'Morning Song' is a love poem, a tribute to the fragility of the new arrival it celebrates. But Plath knows that no mother can make the world safe. If Plath had had her way, the published collection of *Ariel* would not just have opened with this poem whose first word is 'Love'; it would have ended with the poems that have come to be known as the Bee Sequence, the last of which – 'Wintering' – ends on the word 'spring'. Notoriously, Ted Hughes excised the poems that seemed most obviously to allude to the breakdown of their marriage, and ended the collection with later poems written in the days before she died, making her death seem poetically inevitable.[2] But Plath's own carefully laid-out selection was eloquent. Opening with the birth of her child, it allowed joy – love, spring – to be in touch with, and frame, the darkness of shadows. Feminists have rightly objected to the blatant attempt by Hughes to silence Plath's rage as a woman and to exonerate himself (charges given a new edge by the recently uncovered letters from Plath to her former therapist suggesting Hughes had been violent towards her).[3] But today I see his greatest offence as editor of her work residing in the way he curtailed and framed her all-encompassing voice as a mother.

'All I want is for you to be happy.' What mother, parent, would not stand by that appeal, however impossible a demand it must be? First, as the demand to be happy, rather than, say, to be alive in your own life; then, as a kind of vicarious living through one's child; and finally, as most likely the death knell for any chance of happiness, since you surely kill happiness the moment you ask someone to be happy on behalf of anybody else. That same sister once told me with great pleasure how she had found herself on a train talking to a woman who had migrated from the Caribbean in the 1950s and then worked her way through the system, against considerable odds, to become the head teacher in a London school. She threw her head back in a paroxysm of laughter at the suggestion that a parent should want their child to be happy, as if the whole idea was some kind of sick joke, the very last thing a mother should ask for – of – her child. She had the ills of the world at her fingertips, but she was not world-weary, more like jubilant at all that needed to be done. This was in the 1970s, long before her son became one of the most renowned analysts of anti-black racism in the UK and beyond (he did her proud, as one might say).

I always remember that story – its stubborn, expansive generosity of spirit – when I think of the way mothers are expected to lock any feelings of despair behind closed doors, especially in those first precarious moments of a mothering life. Perhaps what goes by the name of 'postnatal depression' is a way of registering griefs past, present and to come, an affront to the ideal not least because of the unbearable weight of historical memory and/or prescience it carries. It has recently been suggested that 'bipolar', with the neat, over-clarifying split it records and enacts as a term, should be replaced with the more old-fashioned 'manic depressive', which at least gives back to the sufferer the dignity of lament, and therefore of potential self-understanding.[4] The term 'postnatal depression' retains the lament but, assigned to hormone imbalance, the condition is now most often treated with drugs, or the quick-fix therapy known as CBT (cognitive behavioural therapy), or in some cases with electroconvulsive therapy, as so graphically described by the novelist Fiona Shaw.[5] It, too, could do with being re-entered into the canon of human distress, psychically and historically meaningful, as opposed to a purely clinical matter.

During a recent visit to South Africa, the incidence of postnatal depression was described to me as 'pandemic', prevalent at the highest rates among the poor blacks, who are, of course, most strongly affected by the unremitting anti-black racism of the country and the persistence of vicious forms of social and economic inequality. A recent South African study focused on depression among low-income black mothers of older children towards whom they found themselves, to their utmost despair, enacting forms of violent rage. When asked how they understood their anger and aggression, they gave three main causes: the demanding child and their longing to be an 'ever-bountiful, ever-giving mother'; the inconsiderate child who made them acutely aware of their own need for attention, support and respect; and the child engaged in violence and drug abuse who thwarted the mother's yearning for 'a new identity and a new life through her child'.[6] Note the mirror-type reflection, or descending spiral, that binds the depressed mother to her child: the child's demands drive the mother to insane perfection; the inconsiderate child underscores the radical neglect of her own life; the violent child destroys the hope for a better future that the child was meant to personify.

As the authors of this study insist, these stories also bear witness to the strong correlation between 'major' depression and poverty, a link that tends to be over-looked clinically, and that must be hugely exacerbated by the promise of a better life with the end of apartheid, a promise that has not materialised for the majority of blacks in South Africa. It also shows these women, long-ing as they were for recognition and support as mothers, repeating an age-old pattern in which a woman's anger, because it is socially unacceptable, is internalised as potential violence against herself and/or her child. But what stood out for me is the vicious circle of ideali-sation inside which these women were trapped. One by one they sourced their rage to 'the pain and disap-pointments associated with not being the mothers they wanted to be'.[7] They felt they had failed because they lashed out at their children; but they lashed out at their children because they felt they had failed. 'Melancholy murderousness' is the title of the study. There can be no clearer example of the self-defeating, violence-inducing character of idealisation as it bears down upon mothers – notably the most disadvantaged and vulnerable mothers – in an unjust world. Yet again we see how, when the world turns ugly, when it cannot bear to confront its own cruelty, the punishing of mothers darkens and intensifies.

*

Throughout this book I have argued against the pernicious weight of the ideal. But it has only been in the course of writing it that I have come to think that the worst, most insufferable demand that so many cultures of the modern world impose on their mothers is not just the saccharine image laid across the mother in expectation of a better future, but the vast reach of historical, political and social anguish that we thereby ask a mother to nullify. We expect her to look to the future (what else is she meant to do?), but the seeming innocence of that expectation is an illusion, as if it were the task of mothers to trample over the past and lift us out of historical time – or, in the version that at least has the virtue of its own sentimentality, to secure a new dawn.

My maternal grandmother's family perished in Chełmno extermination camp during the Second World War. My grandparents in London wanted nothing more than to be safe in their new surroundings, for their two daughters to bear no trace of the atrocity that irredeemably scarred their own lives. But the education of girls formed no part of their vision. Their most fervent wish was for their daughters to get married, to a Jewish man, of course, have children and 'settle down' (an idea that might bear some scrutiny, since, as a therapist once said to me, moments of feeling settled once and for all tend to be life's interruptions). Barely twenty years old, my mother was married off to my father, who was returning from his own trauma, having been tortured in a Japanese prisoner-of-war camp. She had wanted to be a doctor, but was not allowed by her parents to take up the place she had secured at medical school, so she was married to a doctor instead.

Her ambitions for the lives of her own daughters would grow from that thwarted moment and reach for the sky. But, I find myself asking, whatever made her think that this would be enough to silence the past? That educational and sexual freedom – upending the constraints of her life, and for which I will always be grateful – could guarantee a future unstained by that awful history? Maybe there will always be a radical disjunction between what a child is and what a mother most fervently wants for her child. Maybe that is one of the agonies of being a mother: to find that your child harbours in the recesses of their soul a story from which you had hoped against hope, once and for all, to free them. 'With the best will in the world', was one of the sayings I heard repeated throughout my childhood, as if somewhere the grown-ups knew that they were asking – could not help but ask – the impossible of themselves.

When I was a teenager, I came across the account of 'housewives' psychosis' in de Beauvoir's *The Second Sex*. Every morning before we went to school, my sister and I, and eventually our younger sister, were expected to join in the ritual three-cloth cleansing of the entire home: wet, dry and methylated spirits. As I look back on it now, I don't think, as she cleaned the house spotless, that my mother ever realised there was nothing she needed to expiate, that she had not been the perpetrator – not ever, not now nor in the distant past – of any crime. It has become commonplace to describe my mother's generation as housewives without feminism – indeed, it is in response to this post-war closeted domesticity that 1970s second-generation feminism begins. But the point is mostly made without any allusion to the legacy that must have played such a key role in driving them mad. Certainly, no one seems ever to have explained to this generation of housewives and mothers – de Beauvoir did not make the link – that they were not, and should not feel, guilty for a war whose every lingering trace the bright, glittering home in which they had settled down was meant to wipe away for ever.

This book has tried to travel the world and cross epochs – from South Africa to Ancient Greece; from present-day America to slavery and its legacies; from UK post-Brexit to the lines laid down by British policy on mothers after the Second World War; from Naples to Syria. Framing the whole project has been the anguish of mothers and the hostility unleashed against them in response to a crisis of historic proportions that has brought to our shores mothers in search of health support to deliver their babies safely, along with thousands of unaccompanied minors whose mothers might never see them, and who might never see their mothers, again. But I have been writing as the daughter of a white, upper-middle-class mother in post-war Britain whose life is far away from the impoverished black mothers in Cape Town, who fall to pieces when they discover that the violence of their daily lives – the violence they most fear for their children – has entered their hearts, contaminating the very core of what it means for them to be a mother.

In Britain in the 1950s, the instruction a mother should impart to her children, or so it seemed to me as a daughter, was to keep everything in order, up to scratch. Be bold – as daughters we would have the freedoms our mother was denied – but above all hold everything safely in its proper place (the two expectations somewhat contradicting each other). To Gillian's and my bemusement, my mother often said that what she would like most would be to wrap her daughters in cotton wool and glue us to the wall of her bedroom. It was a prospect whose appeal, needless to say, we failed to grasp. The fact that atrocity lurked beneath the veneer and in the attic, that memory could not be so easily subdued, was something not to be spoken (although the cotton wool image is the giveaway, as if she wanted to muffle the sounds).

But none of this was absent from our inner worlds. It is only very recently that my stepmother and I have been able to talk about the disturbance my father suffered for the rest of his days, consequent on what he had seen and endured in Thailand. Only in these past years have I understood that one manifestation of his distress, and one of my most troubling symptoms throughout my life, is something that, with no communication whatsoever between us on the topic, he and I shared. I had missed this connection, partly because I had always assumed, as daughters often do, that any suffering of body or mind I had inherited, in fact pretty much everything I inherited, must have come from my mother. Like a friend of mine who, permanently on the lookout for the first sign in herself of her mother's Alzheimer's, was wholly unprepared, when she suffered a stroke, to find herself afflicted with her father's weak and ailing heart.

The task of a mother, as they say, is to calm the child's fears. But no exhortation to mothers that I have ever read suggests for one moment that her ability to do so might be coloured by fears of her own. Remember North, Colonel Pargiter's grandson, in Virginia Woolf's *The Years*: '*my* boy – *my* girl . . . they were saying. But they're not interested in other people's children, he observed. Only in their own; their own property; their own flesh and blood, which they would protect with the unsheathed claws of the primeval swamp, he thought

. . . how then can we be civilised?'[8] A mother is meant to be as fearless as a lioness. Never mind the brute disregard this implies towards all other children in the world, the children of different class, colour or creed. Nor the unspoken implication that all children are in permanent danger of aggression (a bit of a problem if it is 'civilisation' you think you are talking about).

Even more relevant here is the fact that the image strips the mother of all memory and history, reducing her to an unthinking beast. That this is hardly a fair description of the mental lives of the non-human species of the world is clearly of no concern to North, who therefore sides with the drawing-room refinement he appears to critique. A lioness, it is implied, will instinctively protect her cubs because she has no internal life of her own to grapple with. Push a bit further and you might say that having nothing of her own to grapple with – being 'all' for her child at the cost of her own inner life – is the very definition, or at least the unspoken agenda, of being a mother. This, too, has a long history. For early proponents of 'republican motherhood' in the US in the eighteenth century, the nation's stability depended on the civic virtue a mother cultivated in her child, which required her to be free of all 'invidious and rancorous passions'.[9]

It is, of course, a truism of both feminism and Marxism that the image of stability represented by safe white middle-class homes is a complete myth, resting as such homes do on the exploitation of workers, women and colonies. Just as it is a truism of Freudian thought that the façade of civilised living – in nations Freud referred to, with limited sympathy, as 'the great world-dominating nations of white race' and 'our present-day white Christian culture' – is precarious and phoney in direct proportion to the insistence with which it claims to believe unerringly in itself.[10] 'It goes without saying,' Freud writes in *The Future of an Illusion*, 'that a civilization which leaves so large a number of its participants unsatisfied and drives them into revolt neither has nor deserves the prospect of a lasting existence.'[11] A simpler way of putting this would be to say there is a violence behind the norm, a violence which it is truly a form of insanity to expect mothers – on whatever social rung and wherever they find themselves in the world – to placate. Without question my mother has gifted me with the privilege that her family, refugees from horror, bravely secured for their daughters' sake. But I also know that, against every fibre and bone in her body, she, like my father, has passed on to me a history I sometimes find myself warding off in the night, and which for her part has been too painful, consciously at least, to contemplate. Only once did she tell us of the day – she must have been about nineteen – when she found her mother stretched out on her bed, weeping hysterically, crumpled in her hand the telegram reporting the murder of her entire family in Poland.

*

It is often suggested, in the modern Western world, that the new, improved relationship between mothers and their teenage and/or adult daughters is like that of two especially close girlfriends who share everything: secrets, gossip and clothes (the long-running Netflix series, *Gilmore Girls*, set in 'storybook' Connecticut, about the relationship of Lorelai Gilmore and Rory, her teenage daughter, would be a prime example).[12] As if all secrets were above board, or commodities to be passed round like a shared gourmet dish. When I started down the path of adopting my daughter, the first question on the form I was asked to fill in was: 'What are your family secrets?' I refused to answer it (just one of several moments that nearly brought the whole process to an abrupt halt). Surely, I suggested, a family secret should be respected as such? You would be amazed, the social worker insisted with barely concealed glee, how much invaluable information we get in response to that question. It had not occurred to her that a potential mother who betrays her family secrets as the price to pay for a child cannot be trusted with anything. The assumption was – and this endured throughout the whole process – that minds and hearts are fully open for inspection, that there are no boundaries between what can and cannot be said. This vision of a borderless world was completely contradicted by the obstacles placed in the path of any woman wanting to adopt from overseas, which social services grudgingly accepted while doing everything they could to block and discourage, since it was basically seen as a form of immigration, bringing unwanted future citizens, orphans as they were, to the UK.

Within months of bringing my daughter back from China – to say I was ecstatic would be an understatement – I headed off to Paris to introduce her proudly to some of my oldest, dearest friends, only to be turned back at the airport. I had the adoption papers with me and my baby was now entered in my passport, although she did not yet have a British passport of her own. It had taken more than two years, and an obduracy I had no idea I was capable of, to be accepted as an adopting mother. But this did not stop the border officials announcing they would not let me through as they could not be sure that I was not planning to leave her in France – to abandon an already abandoned baby – as an illegal migrant who might in time start claiming housing and work benefits (she was not yet one year old).

A few days later I waited in a queue at the Home Office to secure permission to travel, surrounded by Africans and Asians, would-be fellow travellers all falling outside the Schengen Agreement that allows free movement between the designated countries of Europe. That agreement has been threatened by the present migration crisis, as if even then, and despite the manifestly racist discrimination of Schengen that I had seen with my own eyes, Europe had failed to police its borders fiercely enough (the borders whose policing will come to be at the heart of the 2016 Brexit vote to leave the EU). When my name was finally called, I was ushered to the front of the queue, only to find, sickeningly, that it was because they had got wind of me as a white, British, professional, tax-paying citizen, unlike the Africans and Asians who, as some of them told me, had been hovering for days on end in the hall.

At the airport, I had wanted to scream at the officials: 'You do not know this baby's history.' But then, I realised, neither – fully – did I. Nor would I, ever. It was and still is a crime to abandon a baby in China, even if the practice was precipitated by the government's own one-child policy that, in the absence of proper pension provision, made parents desperate for a boy whose future wife would tend to them in their later years (whereas a married daughter would leave the home). Which means that, with very few exceptions, none of us who adopted from China in the early 1990s would ever be able to uncover the history of our children, other than being able to tell our daughters over time that their biological parents, far from casually abandoning their infant, had taken the utmost care, and indeed placed themselves at risk of arrest, by leaving her in a public place where she would immediately be found. But, for the most part, my daughter does not know – she has accepted that she cannot know – the story of her own past, although somewhere she must surely be carrying it within her.

Our two founding stories could not be more different, even if a tale of migration shadows both. Yet what each of us is faced with – what any mother, any child, is faced with – is a past that will not yield its secrets willingly or without a struggle, if at all. Mothers and daughters cannot tell each other everything, because they do not know – nobody knows – everything about themselves: not about their own lives, or the secrets of their families, or that part of history weighing on their shoulders that is too hard to communicate. All of which is simply another way of saying that one of the most unrealistic demands made of mothers is that they should be so inhumanly confident and sure of themselves.

Conversations between a mother and child can be as rich as they are unforetold. But the image of a mother and daughter of a certain class giggling over their latest purchases, even, apparently, over the details of their sex lives, is for me a self-deception, complicit with the false cheer, the exhortation to be happy, through which a difficult world buries its true nature. As if mother and daughter alike were meant to behave as a compliant child, the child who, in Winnicott's account, is too scared to be properly ruthless and dare not make proper use of her own mother. Or to put it another way, confidence is a gift, but the version of confidence a mother is mostly asked to instil in her children in the consumer-driven societies of the Western world is based on a pack of lies.

Among its other problems, the exhortation to be happy is, literally, a killjoy. Joy is not always possible. Like all forms of intimacy, it relies on at least a modicum of freedom. In relation to mothers, joy – as in 'the joys of motherhood' – can be a corrupt term. Buchi Emecheta's ironically named novel *The Joys of Motherhood* (1979) opens with a mother whose tribulations in a polygamous Nigerian tribal community have driven her to attempt suicide.[13] But if joy is a privilege, it is also something for which you cannot prepare yourself, as though it were a garment that you first try on for size; unlike happiness, which tends to present itself as a habit of mind, devoutly to be wished, a prize possession to be sought and gained, an achievement or resting place.[14]

None of this comes near the radical disorientation of joy, certainly nowhere near the experience I have had as a mother. Resting in the afternoon while my baby was asleep, in the days after bringing her home, I would suddenly jolt awake at the sensation that she was lying on top of me, only to realise that she was in fact inside me – a close-on crazy thought of overwhelming delight – whereupon I would drift back into sleep. I was going through an inverse pregnancy, moving backwards in time, letting her in, or rather, it felt, her claiming her place as she crawled inside my body and into my blood-stream. Had anyone told me in advance that this was an experience common to adopting mothers – not that I had heard of it before or indeed have I since – I have no doubt I would have lain awake waiting, fruitlessly, for it to happen.

I was being turned inside out. This, I suggest, is the chief property of joy, certainly of maternal joy, which shatters the carapace of selfhood. Nor is it restricted to mothering alone. I have a friend who, with great reluctance, sent packing her passionate married lover of several years because, in the end, she could not bear him heading off after lovemaking of such intensity that she felt her body was opening to the winds, each and every nerve raw to the elements, something she had not known since giving birth to her two children more than ten years ago. And before being shocked at this analogy, we might remember the erotic charge of breastfeeding as one of the best-kept secrets of mothering (and Freud's suggestion that the prototype for all later sexual pleasure was the sated baby at the mother's breast).

'The child brings joy,' writes Simone de Beauvoir, 'only to the woman who is capable of disinterestedly desiring the happiness of another, to one who without reversion to herself, seeks to go beyond her own experience.'[15] Joy is not, as we have seen, a word most readily associated with the writing of de Beauvoir, certainly not in relation to motherhood. But here, in one of its rare appearances, it is clearly describing a form of dispossession. Whether in sexual passion, giving birth or being a mother, joy is fleeting, as they say, not so much because it doesn't last, as because you can only experience it by letting go of something else. This is not, however, some idea of maternal sacrifice – the last thing de Beauvoir would ever promote or advocate. Remember that, in her eyes, it was a fatal mistake for a mother to believe she must do, and be, 'all' for her child (the flip side of this delusion is thinking you own your child, which turns a mother into a man asserting his property rights). It was, after all, the judgement of Solomon that the true mother was the one who would release her baby to a false claimant rather than tear the baby in two – an act that, one might argue, only a bereaved mother who had already lost her child would, in a fit of jealous rage, insanely contemplate.

In the hands of de Beauvoir, I suggested, motherhood became the place where a philosophy in thrall to self-mastery reached its limits and started to disintegrate. In this de Beauvoir is not far from Elena Ferrante, whose vision of motherhood, out of which for her all writing is born, dissolves the world's borders. As a child, Ferrante had watched her mother fall to pieces physically and mentally under the pressures of being a wife and mother. Seizing on such moments, Ferrante transmutes them into an erotic, cosmic dreamscape: 'a swarm of bees approaching above the motionless treetops; the sudden eddy in a slow body of water . . . a bright-coloured explosion of sounds . . . of butterflies with sonorous wings.'[16] But, we should recall, it was only by plunging into a world that has lost all contour and plays havoc with decency – a world to which Ferrante's mothers have their own special access – that she was able to produce such moments of ecstasy in her writing.

To all of these questions of boundaries and possession adoption gives its own unique hue. An adopting mother knows somewhere deep down that she does not own her child, something I have always seen as a caution, a truth and a gift. Not everyone, of course, is of the same view. 'How could you do it?' one friend asked me as he clutched his newborn to his chest. 'I wanted,' he admitted with just a touch of embarrassment, 'to see my DNA grow and spread, my biological heritage and all that.' 'But to nurture another's baby is to be part of the DNA of the whole world,' I retorted, with perhaps an unfortunate tinge of self-righteousness. 'My daughter and I belong as much to the biology and growing of the earth as you.' The question, as we have seen so many times, is who you feel linked to and where you draw the line. During the adoption process we had to engage in role play, at one point being asked to imagine ourselves as the biological mother of our future baby. One man – older, with a very young wife – refused. 'What has she got to do with us?' he asked. 'After all, she left her baby. Why should I think or care about her?' From where we were in the process, I knew that the baby who would come to be my daughter was most likely about to be born, to a mother who would leave her through no fault

of her own. I also knew that, faced with the abandonment of a baby girl, as a feminist I should fume and fret
and rage. 'I think about her every day,' I replied. Even
though her act would allow me – joyously – to become
the mother I had always wanted to be, as I spoke all I
felt was sorrow.

*

To finish with two moments taken from opposite ends
of the earth.

In the early 1990s, at the Kaiser Medical Center, Los
Angeles, Susan Stryker, trans activist and writer, held
her pregnant lover between her spread legs as she gave
birth, gripping Stryker so hard that she left bruises on
her thigh. As she felt a child move out of another woman's body, 'a jumble of dark unsolicited feelings' emerged
'wordlessly from some back corner' of her mind.[17] The
medical staff were clueless as to how the various members of this 'little tribe' all related to each other: mother,
biological father, their personal midwife, the mother's
sister, Stryker and her son from an earlier heterosexual
– sort of – marriage. 'Step by increasingly intimate step,'
Stryker found herself participating in the ritual of trans-
forming consciousness that heralded this new birth, 'a
profound opening, as psychic as it is corporeal'.[18] When
she later returned to her home, she burst open – opening
is key – 'like a wet paper bag', spilling the 'emotional

contents of my life through the hands I cupped like a sieve over my face'.[19] It is agony, not least because of the mourning it provokes for the earlier marriage that had produced her son. But it is also 'simple joy bubbling out, wave after wave', as well as a moment of total dispossession, not unlike others we have seen, as she prepares 'to let go of whatever was deepest within'.[20]

It is an extraordinary piece of writing, a tribute to the moment of giving birth as an experience into which anyone can enter, can lose and find themselves. Perhaps – although Stryker herself does not quite say this – it is only the radical disorientation of transgender that makes such an exuberant and painful crossing possible. Far from the air-brushed, sanitised image of mothering we have so often seen, and miles from the world of entrenched borders, which is where this book started, Stryker suggests that, in relation to this founding act of motherhood, what matters is how close you can get. Another way of putting this is that in an ideal world, everyone, whatever the impulses driving them hard and fast in the opposite direction, would be capable of thinking of themselves as mothers.

Sindiwe Magona's novel *Mother to Mother* (1998) offers a no less unprecedented crossing of paths in the name of mothers, though it belongs to a different world. We last encountered Magona through her story of the mother who, driven from her home in search of work under apartheid, had to abandon her babies. A few years later, in 1993, with the end of apartheid barely a year away, the young white American campaigner and human rights activist Amy Biehl was killed in the township of Gugulethu, to the cry of 'One settler, one bullet!' Her death sent shock waves through the community, indeed throughout the country as a whole, although it was impossible not to register that it was her whiteness that made her killing – unlike the untold deaths of blacks across the nation – such an outrage. Gugulethu was Magona's township. *Mother to Mother*, her acclaimed first novel, is imagined from the point of view of the mother of the boy who was indicted for the killing, and addresses itself to the mother of Amy Biehl. Far from the domestic cosiness ironically coded in the title (*From Mother to Mother: Recipes from a Family Kitchen* is the title of a cookbook published in the US in 2017), Magona is asking a question as if the future of her nation, and not just her nation, depended on it: how could two such different mothers possibly listen, or have anything to say, to each other?

I end with this book because it condenses so many of the themes that have been my focus here. It places motherhood firmly in the context of a material life, scarred with a history of racial inequality and injustice (the forced removal of the Cape blacks to Gugulethu in 1958 forms the historical background to the novel). It gives a mother the right to her own memories and the complexity of her inner mind, even when that includes the unbearable thought that, as well as loving, she has always hated her son. First, because of the agonies of his birth – 'pain with the savageness of the jaws of a shark' – which then, only a few moments later, transmutes into the most intense love and joy: 'all infusing light-headedness . . . Joy, pure and simple.'[21] And then in response to the loss of her own educational ambitions, ambitions that she had passionately nurtured until she became a wife and mother, when – abandoned by the father of her child – they turned to dust. From the moment of his conception, her son, Mxolisi, is sheer upheaval: 'his implanting himself inside me; unreasonably and totally destroying the me I was'.[22] (At moments like these, the novel reads like an updated, politically and racially inflected version of Winnicott's eighteen reasons a mother has to hate her baby.)

Tracing the inhumanity of the apartheid regime, she gives her son's violent act – which she abhors – the dignity of a history. But she also tracks his troubled soul, thereby holding both history and his own uniquely personal trajectory to account in one and the same breath (as if to say: it is the responsibility of an unjust world, it is also mine). Her son was the 'sharpened arrow of the wrath of his race', but he was also a boy who as a child had once betrayed his dearest friends during a police raid on their homes, and who then went mute for more than two years after he stood there watching as the two boys were dragged out and shot.[23]

This mother is also a dissenter, deeply attuned to the political dilemmas of her life. You could say that, even if it is the last thing she would have wished for, the public nature of her life as a mother is what the killing brings home to her. She is fierce in her critique of the township necklacing of those believed to be collaborators with the apartheid regime; she rejects the cry that all whites are dogs. And her body, the maternal body we have so often seen either degraded or refined out of existence in the popular imagination, is made palpable on the page, when she is giving birth, and then again – no less powerfully – when, walking into her shack, it dawns on her that her son is the killer: 'Slowly, carefully, my body gone all liquid, I watched myself pour it onto the chair.'[24] Remember Sethe, in Toni Morrison's *Beloved*, running round the side of the house to empty her bladder when she first recognises the ghost of the baby daughter she had murdered, rather than allow her to be enslaved. Remember, again, the mother from Magona's earlier story, expressing her breast milk onto the track. And Stryker, worlds apart, cupping her hands like a sieve over her face.

Throughout all this, the narrator maintains the conversation between herself and the mother of Amy Biehl. The novel *is* that conversation:

> Your daughter. The imperfect atonement of her race.
> My son. The perfect host of the demons of his.[25]

Her task as a mother is to call up the legacy of her child, and – across barriers human and inhuman – the legacy of the dead child whose mother is facing her. Near the end of the novel, she addresses her interlocutor even more directly: 'But now, my Sister-Mother, do I help him hide? Deliver him to the police? Get him a lawyer? Will that mean I do not feel your sorrow for your slain daughter? Am I your enemy? Are you mine? What wrong have I done you . . . or you me?'[26]

There are, of course, no simple answers to these questions. There is no false reconciliation. This is not a mother tasked with historical and political redemption.[27] But merely by asking them, Magona is giving voice to a problem that resonates throughout this book. How to get such stories into the mainstream version of what it means to be a mother, and into the narrative of what mothers might be for each other? What would happen, finally if, instead of asking mothers to appease the wrongs of history and the heart, and then punishing them when they inevitably fail, we listen to what they have to say – from deep within their bodies and minds – about both? Perhaps it would indeed bring the world to an end as we know it, but I suspect, certainly for mothers, this would be no bad thing.

CODA

When I was preparing to adopt my daughter, I would try to seduce my social worker with obscenely large red cherries, which would sit in their bowl, I liked to think, as a flagrant riposte to and distraction from her steely, relentless inquisition (the adoption process raises the idea of a fault-finding mission to a new height). I remember thinking later that the two things the whole process could never prepare you for, and which made it as useless as it was invasive, were first, the worry – the OMG of every scratch and fall, at once absurd and wholly in tune with the fragility of life – and second, the joy. In the famous story, Tiresias is struck blind by Hera, in some versions by Athena, for having revealed that a woman's sexual pleasure is greater than a man's. As I was thinking about motherhood in our time and reading all the outpourings on the subject, past and present, that story came to mind. We need a version for mothers, one in which the acute pleasure of being a mother, without any need for denial of everything else talked about here, would be neither a guilty secret, nor something enviously co-opted by bullies – 'You *will* be happy!' Instead, it could be left to get on quietly with its work of making the experience of motherhood more than worth it.

ACKNOWLEDGEMENTS

When the *London Review of Books* invited me to write a piece on mothers, none of us, least of all me, had any notion of where it might lead. This book is the 'offspring' of the article 'Mothers' published in the *LRB* on 19 June 2014 (36:12). So my first thanks go to Mary-Kay Wilmers for the idea and to Paul Myerscough for his, as always, scrupulous editing. Thanks to Mitzi Angel at Faber and Eric Chinski at Farrar, Straus and Giroux for persuading me that this topic could, or should, be a book, for their encouragement, and to Mitzi especially for her editorial attention and care. I am fortunate to have Tracy Bohan as agent, and much appreciate her unfailing enthusiasm, perception and kindness.

The book has been written since I had the privilege of joining the Birkbeck Institute for the Humanities in 2015. I am indebted to Esther Leslie and Madisson Brown for their solidarity and support. My visits to the Institute for Social Justice at the Australian Catholic University in Sydney have also provided a stimulating intellectual backdrop to the book.

Cora Kaplan, Sally Alexander, Alison Rose and

Elizabeth Karlsen have read all or part of the manuscript, each with their customary fine eye and insight. I am grateful to Edith Hall and to Esther Eidinow for their comments on chapter 2. All remaining errors are, of course, my own. Mia Rose made some crucial corrections to the final chapter, key moments of which she also inspired.

A number of friends and acquaintances provided one or more of the anecdotes scattered throughout the book, where they remain unnamed. In the hope that it will not lead to a flurry of detective activity, it seems right to name them here (in no particular order, as they say): Lisa Appignanesi, Selma Dabbagh, Livia Griffiths, Katie Fleming, Monique Plaza, Lawrence Jacobsen, Braham Murray. One other gave me much in body and spirit, for which I am thankful. Gillian Rose is more present in this book than I could have imagined when I started writing it.

The book is dedicated to my mother, Lynn Rose, and my stepmother, Jeanette Stone, with whom it all, or so much of it, began.

London, July 2017

NOTES

SOCIAL PUNISHMENT: NOW

1 Amelia Gentleman, 'Fear of bills and Home Office keeping pregnant migrants away from NHS', *Guardian*, 20 March 2017.

2 Amelia Gentleman, Lisa O'Carroll, 'Home Office stops transfer of Calais child refugees to UK', *Guardian*, 10 December 2016; Diane Taylor, 'UK turns back hundreds of refugees', *Guardian*, 17 December 2017; Alan Travis, 'PM accused of closing doors on child refugees', *Guardian*, 9 February 2017.

3 Bernard Cazeneuve, 'The UK must fulfil its moral duty to Calais's unaccompanied children', *Guardian*, 17 October 2016.

4 Lisa O'Carroll, 'Teenagers' stories', *Guardian*, 28 October 2016.

5 Personal communication, Sue Clayton, award-winning independent documentary film-maker, whose crowd-funded film, *Calais Children: A Case to Answer*, was released in June 2017 (footage from the film was aired on ITV and *Channel 4 News*).

6 Diane Taylor, 'Samir, 17, thought he was finally about to reach the UK. Now he's dead', *Guardian*, 19 January 2017.

7 Bertolt Brecht, 'Appendix A: Writing the Truth: Five Difficulties', in *Galileo*, trans. Charles Laughton (New York: Grove Press, 1966), p. 139.

8 Colm Tóibín, *The Testament of Mary* (London: Viking, 2012), p. 102.

9 Judith Shklar, *The Faces of Injustice* (New Haven: Yale, 1994), chapter 2, 'Misfortune and Injustice'.

10 All quotes from Gillian Slovo with Nicolas Kent, *Another World: Losing our Children to Islamic State* (London: Oberon, 2016).

11 Angela McRobbie, 'Feminism, the Family and the New "Mediated" Maternalism', *New Formations* (special issue, 'Neoliberal Culture'), 80/81, 2013; 'Notes on the Perfect: Competitive Femininity in Neoliberal Times', *Australian Feminist Studies*, 30:83, 2015.

12 Sandra Laville, 'Revealed: the secret abuse of women in the family courts', *Guardian*, 23 December 2016.

13 Denis Campbell, 'Female doctors may be forced to quit over new contract, experts say', *Guardian*, 1 April 2016.

14 Nina Gill, 'The new junior doctors' contract is blatantly sexist – so why doesn't Jeremy Hunt care?' *Daily Telegraph*, 4 April 2016.

15 Alexandra Topping, 'Maternity leave discrimination means 54,000 women lose their jobs each year', *Guardian*, 24 July 2015.

16 Karen McVeigh, 'MPs urge action to fight "shocking" bias against mothers', *Guardian*, 31 August 2016.

17 Joeli Brearley and Greg Clark MP: 'Give new and expectant mothers six months to pursue discrimination claims', Change.org, 4 March 2017.

18 Press Association, 'New mothers "facing increasing workplace discrimination"', *Guardian*, 2 May 2016.

19 Karen McVeigh, 'MPs urge action'; Rowena Mason, 'Review of law to protect pregnant women's jobs', *Guardian*, 26 January 2017.

20 Grace Chang, 'Undocumented Latinas: The New "Employable" Mothers', in *Mothering: Ideology, Experience, and Agency*, ed. Evelyn Nakano Glenn, Grace Chang and Linda Rennie Forcey (London: Routledge, 1994), p. 273.

21 Bryce Covert, 'Woman allegedly fired for being pregnant after boss told her "pregnancy is not part of the uniform"', *Think Progress*, 4 May 2016, https://thinkprogress.org/woman-allegedly-fired-for-being-pregnant-after-boss-told-her-pregnancy-is-not-part-of-the-uniform-4d11d29a2c24#.gaajkhtxn.

22 http://www.maternityaction.org.uk/wp-content/uploads/WomenandEqualitiesCommInquiryEv2016.pdf.

23 Sarah Boseley, 'British maternity pay is among worst in Europe', *Guardian*, 24 March 2017.

24 T. J. Matthews, Marian F. MacDorman and Marie E. Thomas, 'Infant mortality statistics from the 2013 period: linked birth/infant data set', *National Vital Statistics Reports*, 64:9, 6 August 2015.

25 Centre for Maternal and Child Enquiries, cited in Hattie Garlick, 'Labour of love', *Guardian* magazine, 17 December 2016.

26 John Donne, 'Death's Duell', in *The Sermons of John Donne*, ed. Theodore Gill (New York: Meridian, 1958), p. 265, cited in Janet Adelman, *Suffocating Mothers: Fantasies of Maternal Origin in Shakespeare's Plays*, Hamlet *to* The Tempest (London: Routledge, 1992), p. 6.

27 Nicholas Kristoff, 'If Americans Love Moms, Why Do We Let Them Die?' *New York Times*, 29 July 1917. See also Nina Martin, Emma Cillekens and Alessandra Freitas, ProPublica, 17 July 2017.

https://www.propublica.org/article/lost-mothers-maternal-health-died-childbirth-pregnancy. Thanks to Eric Chinski for drawing my attention to Kristoff's article.

28 Ibid.

29 Adrienne Rich, *Of Woman Born: Motherhood as Experience and Institution* (New York: Norton 1976, 1995), p. 11 (emphasis original).

30 Ben Morgan, 'Netmums founder tells advertisers: Stop peddling the myth of the perfect mother,' *Evening Standard*, 11 September 2017.

31 Kirsten Andersen, 'The number of US children living in single-parent homes has nearly doubled in 50 years: Census data', *LifeSite News*, 4 January 2013, https://www.lifesitenews.com/news/the-number-of-children-living-in-single-parent-homes-has-nearly-doubled-in.

32 Pat Thane and Tanya Evans, *Sinners? Scroungers? Saints?: Unmarried Motherhood in Twentieth-Century England* (Oxford: OUP, 2012), p. 4.

33 Michelle Harrison, cited in Diana Ginn, 'The Supreme Court of Canada and What It Means to Be "Of Woman Born"', in *From Motherhood to Mothering: The Legacy of Adrienne Rich's Of Woman Born*, ed. Andrea O'Reilly (Albany, NY SUNY Press, 2004), p. 36.

34 Polly Toynbee, 'Our future is being stolen. Be brave and take it back', *Guardian*, 20 December 2016.

35 Thane and Evans, p. 5; Kirsten Andersen.

36 Pat Thane, 'Happy Families? History and Family Policy', British Academy Policy Centre, 2010.

37 Harriet Sherwood, 'Catholic church apologises for role in "forced adoptions" over 30-year period', *Guardian*, 3 November 2016.

38 Patricia Hill Collins, 'Shifting the Center: Race, Class, and Feminist Theorizing about Motherhood', in Glenn, Chang and Forcey.

39 Chang, 'Undocumented Latinas'.

40 Thane and Evans, pp. 16–17.

41 Ibid., p. 69.

42 Ibid.

43 Ibid., p. 77.

44 Gail Lewis, 'Birthing Racial Difference: Conversations with My Mother and Others', *Studies in the Maternal*, 1:1, 2009, pp. 1–21.

45 Thane and Evans, p. 3.

46 Elisabeth Badinter, *The Conflict: How Modern Motherhood Undermines the Status of Women*, trans. Adriana Hunter (New York: Metropolitan Books, 2012), p. 150.

47 Laurie Penny, 'Women shouldn't apologise for the pitter-patter of tiny carbon footprints', *Guardian*, 28 July 2017.

SOCIAL PUNISHMENT: THEN

1 Angeliki Tzanetou, 'Citizen-Mothers on the Tragic Stage', in *Mothering and Motherhood in Ancient Greek and Rome*, ed. Lauren Hackworth Petersen and Patricia Salzman-Mitchell (Austin: University of Texas Press, 2012); Paul Cartledge, '"Deep Plays": Theatre as Process in Greek Civic Life', in *The Cambridge Companion to Greek Tragedy*, ed. P. E. Easterling (Cambridge: CUP, 1997).

2 Cynthia Patterson, 'Citizenship and Gender in the Ancient World', in *Migrations and Mobilities: Citizenship, Borders and Gender*, ed. Seyla Benhabib and Judith Resnik (New York University Press, 2009), p. 55.

3 Patterson, 'Citizenship and Gender', p. 60.

4 Barbara Goff, *Citizen Bacchae: Women's Ritual Practice in Ancient Greece* (Oakland: University of California Press, 2004), pp. 2–5.

5 Cynthia Patterson, 'Hai Attikai: The Other Athenians', in *Rescuing Creusa: New Methodological Approaches to Women in Antiquity*, ed. Marilyn Skinner, special issue of *Helios*, 13:2, 1986, p. 61.

6 Goff, p. 29, p. 49, p. 61.

7 Rachel Cusk, *A Life's Work: On Becoming a Mother* (London: Fourth Estate, 2001), p. 131.

8 Melissa Benn, *Madonna and Child: Towards a New Politics of Motherhood* (London: Jonathan Cape, 1998), p. 19.

9 Linda Colley, *Britons: Forging the Nation, 1707–1837*, 4th edn (New Haven: Yale, 2009), p. 267, cited in Shaul Bar-Haim, *The Maternalizing Movement: Psychoanalysis, Motherhood and the British Welfare State c. 1920–1950*, unpublished PhD thesis, Birkbeck 2015, p. 20.

10 Patterson, 'Citizenship and Gender', p. 52.

11 Edith Hall, *Introducing the Ancient Greeks* (Oxford: Bodley Head, 2015), p. 7.

12 Goff, p. 5.

13 Hall, p. 7. Also, D. Harvey, 'Women in Thucydides', *Arethusa* 18 (1985), pp. 67–90.

14 Ibid.

15 Mary Beard, *The Parthenon* (London: Profile, 2010), p. 43; Esther Eidinow, *Envy, Poison, and Death: Women on Trial in Classical Athens* (Oxford: OUP, 2016), p. 13.

16 Hackworth Petersen and Salzman-Mitchell, p. 12.

17 Euripides, *The Suppliant Women, Euripides II*, ed. David Grene and Richmond Lattimore (Chicago: University of Chicago Press, 2012), ll. 293–94, p. 151.

18 Ibid., ll. 405–9, p. 157.

19 Nadia Latif and Leila Latif, 'We had to change pain to purpose', interviews with the mothers of Trayvon Martin, Sandra Bland, Eric Garner, Amadou Diallo and Sean Bell, *Guardian*, 22 November 2016.

20 Euripides, *The Suppliant Women*, ll. 767–68.

21 Hannah Arendt, *The Human Condition* (Chicago: University of Chicago Press, 1958), p. 27.

22 *New Society*, cited in Mary-Kay Wilmers, 'Views', *Listener*, May 1972; according to the *Modern Families Index*, 2017, fathers who choose to spend more time with their families are now suffering a 'fatherhood penalty' in relation to their careers. Cited in Jamie Doward, 'It used to be a feminist cause – but now both men and women struggle to thrive at work and still find time for their families.' Jamie Doward, '"Fatherhood penalty" now a risk for men, warns charity,' *Observer*, 15 January 2017.

23 Kathleen Connors, letter to the *London Review of Books*, 36:14, 17 July 2014.

24 Euripides, *The Suppliant Women*, ll. 825–26.

25 Ibid., l. 824.

26 Hall, p. 170.

27 Nicoletta Gullace, *The Blood of Our Sons: Men, Women and the Regeneration of British Citizenship During the Great War* (Basingstoke: Palgrave Macmillan, 2002), pp. 55–59, cited in Bar-Haim, *The Maternalizing Movement*, p. 21.

28 Euripides, *Medea*, trans. Oliver Taplin, *Euripides I*, ed. David Grene and Richmond Lattimore (Chicago: University of Chicago Press, 2013), ll. 250–53, 1091–1116.

29 Ibid., ll. 233–34, 277–78, 231.

30 All quotes from Nicole Loraux, 'Le Lit, la guerre', *L'Homme*, 21:1, January–March 1981.

31 Janet Adelman, *Suffocating Mothers: Fantasies of Maternal Origin in Shakespeare's Plays,* Hamlet to The Tempest (London: Routledge, 1992).

32 Shakespeare, *Coriolanus*, Arden Shakespeare edn (London: Methuen, 1976), Act 1, Sc iii, ll. 40ff.

33 Margaret L. Woodhull, 'Imperial Mothers and Monuments in Rome', in Petersen and Salzman-Mitchell.

34 Philip Brockbank, 'Introduction', in *Coriolanus*, p. 42.

35 Ibid., Act 1, Sc iii, ll. 2–4.

36 Ibid., Act 1, Sc iii, ll. 21–25.

37 Ibid., Act 5, Sc iii, l. 103.

38 Adrienne Rich, *Of Woman Born: Motherhood as Experience and Institution* (New York: Norton 1976, 1995), p. 279.

39 Sarah Boseley, Ruth Maclean and Liz Ford, 'How one of Trump's first acts signed death warrants for women all round the world', *Guardian*, 21 July 2017.

40 Karen McVeigh, 'Reversal of abortion funding puts $9bn health at risk – campaigners', *Guardian*, 25 January 2017.

41 All quotes from Diana Ginn, 'The Supreme Court of Canada and What It Means to Be "Of Woman Born"', in *From Motherhood to Mothering: The Legacy of Adrienne Rich's* Of Woman Born, ed. Andrea O'Reilly (Albany, NY: SUNY Press, 2004), p. 29.

42 *Dobson v. Dobson*, cited Ginn, p. 33.

43 Tess Cosslett, *Women Writing Childbirth: Modern Discourses of Motherhood* (Manchester University Press, 1994), p. 119, cited in Ginn, p. 38.

44 *Dobson v. Dobson*, cited Ginn, p. 39

45 Jacques Guillimeau, *The Nursing of Children, affixed to Childbirth, or the Happy Delivery of Women* (London: printed by Anne Griffin, for Joyce Norton and Richard Whitaker, 1635), cited in Adelman, p. 6.

46 Ibid., Preface 1.i.2; also Audrey Eccles, *Obstetrics and Gynaecology in Tudor and Stuart England* (Kent, Ohio: Kent University Press, 1982), pp. 51–2, cited in Adelman, p. 7.

47 Aeschylus, *The Oresteian Trilogy*, trans. Philip Vellacott (Harmondsworth: Penguin, 1974), Part III, *Eumenides*, ll. 656–61 (emphasis mine)

48 Ibid., ll. 109–10.

49 Ibid., ll. 605–7.

50 Sophocles, *Electra, II*, ll. 532–33, cited in Rachel Bowlby, *Freudian Mythologies: Greek Tragedy and Modern Identities* (Oxford: OUP, 2007), p. 211.

51 My thanks to Edith Hall for this information.

52 Robert Icke, adaptation of Sophocles' *Oresteia* (London: Oberon, 2015), p. 119.

53 Ibid., p. 60.

54 Ibid., p. 118.

55 See Amber Jacobs, *On Matricide: Myth, Psychoanalysis and the Law of the Mother* (New York: Columbia University Press, 2007), for the fullest reckoning with this story and its implications.

56 Aeschylus, *Agamemnon*, ll. 117–20.

57 Colm Tóibín, *House of Names* (London: Viking, 2017).

58 André Green, *Un Œil en trop: Le Complexe d'Œdipe dans la tragédie* (Paris: Minuit, 1969), trans. p. 80 cited in Jacobs.

59 Rachel Bowlby, *A Child of One's Own: Parental Stories* (Oxford: OUP, 2013), p. 114.

60 Elena Ferrante, citing Elsa Morante, 'Mothers' Dressmakers', in *Frantumaglia: A Writer's Journey* (New York: Europa, 2016), p. 17.

61 *Hamlet*, First Quarto, 1603, 11, 53–54.

62 *Hamlet*, First Folio, 1623, 3. iv. 15–16.

63 Ibid., 3. iv. 166.

64 Icke, p. 117.

65 Genevieve Lively, 'Mater Amoris: Mothers and Lovers in Augustan Rome', in Hackworth Petersen and Salzman-Mitchell, p. 197.

66 Patricia Salzman-Mitchell, 'Tenderness or Taboo: Images of Breast-Feeding Mothers in Greek and Latin Literature', in Hackworth Petersen and Salzman-Mitchell, pp. 150–51.

67 Martin Bernal, *Black Athena: The Afroasiatic Roots of Classical Civilisation, Volume I, The Fabrication of Ancient Greece* (New Jersey: Rutgers University Press, 1987).

68 Rhiannon Stephens, *A History of African Motherhood: The Case of Uganda, 700–1900* (Cambridge: CUP, 2013).

69 Nicole Loraux, *Mothers in Mourning*, trans. Corinne Pache (Ithaca: Cornell University Press, 1998), p. 51.

70 Euripides, *Medea*, Introduction, p. 70.

71 Ibid., ll. 1366, 1368–69, p. 130.

72 Ibid., ll. 1060–62, p. 117.

73 Véronique Olmi, *Bord de mer/Beside the Sea*, trans. Adriana Hunter (London: Peirene, 2010), p. 68.

74 Margaret Reynolds, 'Performing Medea: or, Why Is Medea a Woman?', in *Medea in Performance, 1500–2000*, ed. Edith Hall, Fiona Macintosh and Oliver Taplin (Oxford: Legenda, 2000), p. 139, p. 140.

75 Christa Wolf, *Medea: A Modern Retelling*, trans. John Cullen (London: Virago, 1998), p. 7.

76 Ibid., pp. 111–13.

77 Ibid., p. 80.

78 Ibid.

79 Rich, p. 270.

80 W. G. Sebald, *On the Natural History of Destruction*, trans. Anthea Bell (London: Hamish Hamilton, 2003), p. 13.

81 Wolf, pp. 1–2.

PSYCHIC BLINDNESS: LOVING

1 Roald Dahl, *Matilda* (London: Jonathan Cape, 1988; Puffin, 2013), p. 4.

2 Adrienne Rich, *Of Woman Born: Motherhood as Experience and Institution* (New York: Norton 1986, 1995), p. xxxiii.

3 Hannah Arendt, *The Origins of Totalitarianism* (New York: Harcourt Brace Jovanovich, 1979), p. 473.

4 Ibid.

5 Virginia Woolf, *The Years*, 1937 (Oxford: OUP, 1992), p. 359 (emphasis mine).

6 Rachel Cusk, *A Life's Work: On Becoming a Mother* (London: Fourth Estate, 2001), p. 8.

7 Ibid., p. 137.

8 Rich, p. xxiv.

9 Mary-Kay Wilmers, 'Views', *Listener*, May 1972.

10 Denise Riley, *War in the Nursery: Theories of the Child and Mother* (London: Virago, 1983).

11 Luise Eichenbaum and Susie Orbach, *Understanding Women: A Feminist Psychoanalytic Approach* (London: Penguin, 1985); Rozsika Parker, *Torn in Two: The Experience of Maternal Ambivalence* (London: Virago, 1995); and Lisa Baraitser, *Maternal Encounters: The Ethics of Interruption* (London: Routledge, 2009). Baraitser is also co-founder of MaMSIE (Mapping Maternal Subjectivities, Identities and Ethics), a network based in the Department of Psychosocial Studies at Birkbeck University of London, which publishes the journal *Studies in the Maternal*.

12 Michel Onfray, *Théorie du corps amoureux* (Paris: LGF, 2007), p. 219–20, cited in Elisabeth Badinter, *The Conflict: How Modern Motherhood Undermines the Status of Women*, trans. Adriana Hunter (New York: Metropolitan Books, 2012), p. 125.

13 Badinter, p. 69.

14 Ibid., pp. 67–84.

15 Ibid., p. 73.

16 Haroon Siddique, 'Less than half of women breastfeed after two months', *Guardian*, 23 March 2017.

17 Hadley Freeman, 'Never let me go', *Guardian* magazine, 30 July 2016.

18 Jake Dypka and Hollie McNish, 'Embarrassed', Channel 4, Random Acts, https://www.youtube.com/watch?v=S6nHrqIFTj8. In 2017, McNish won the Ted Hughes Award. McNish: 'I always attracted mums and midwives, Now I get poetry lovers.' *Guardian*, 16 June 2017. See also Rachel Epp Buller, 'Performing the Breastfeeding Body: Lactivism

and Art Intervention', *Studies in the Maternal*, 8:2, 2016, p. 14.

19 Letters, *London Review of Books*, 36:14, 17 July 2014.

20 Helene Deutsch, 'The Psychology of Woman in Relation to the Functions of Reproduction', 1925, in Robert Fliess, *The Psychoanalytic Reader* (New York: International Universities Press, 1969).

21 Wilmers, 'Views'.

22 Courtney Love, 'Plump', 'Softest, Softest', 'I Think That I Would Die'. Thanks to Barry Schwabsky for alerting me to these lyrics.

23 *Toni Morrison*, Icon Critical Guides, ed. Carl Plasa (Cambridge, MA: Icon Books, 1998), p. 36.

24 Toni Morrison, *Beloved* (London: Chatto & Windus, 1987), p. 51.

25 Ibid., p. 209.

26 See also Saidiya Hartman, *Lose Your Mother: A Journey Along the Atlantic Slave Route* (New York: Farrar, Straus and Giroux, 2007).

27 Stephanie J. Shaw, 'Mothering under Slavery in the Antebellum South', in *Mothering: Ideology, Experience, and Agency*, ed. Evelyn Nakano Glenn, Grace Chang and Linda Rennie Forcey (London: Routledge, 1994), p. 249.

28 Patricia Hill Collins, 'The Meaning of Motherhood in Black Culture and Black Mother–Daughter Relationships', in *Double Stitch: Black Women Write About Mothers and Daughters* (New York: Beacon Press, 1991), p. 53.

29 Ibid., p. 8.

30 Sindiwe Magona, *Living, Loving, and Lying Awake at Night* (Claremont, South Africa: David Philip, 1991), p. 5.

31 Ibid., p. 6.

32 Ibid., p. 7.

33 Ibid., p. 16.

34 Hermione Lee, *Edith Wharton* (London: Chatto & Windus, 2007).

35 Edith Wharton, *The Mother's Recompense*, 1925 (Teddington: Wildhern Press, 2008), p. 33.

36 Ibid., p. 7.

37 Ibid., p. 9.

38 Ibid., p. 30.

39 Cited in Lee, p. 627.

40 Lee, p. 330.

41 Wharton, p. 34.

42 Ibid., p. 66.

43 Rich, p. 252.

44 Wharton, pp. 101–2.

45 Ibid., p. 46.
46 Lee, p. 630.
47 Ibid., p. 110, p. 127.
48 Ibid., p. 110.
49 Ibid., p. 110, p. 120.
50 Ibid., p. 123, p. 83.
51 Ibid., p. 97.
52 Ibid., p. 77.
53 Ibid., p. 131.
54 Ariel Leve, *An Abbreviated Life* (New York: HarperCollins, 2016),
   p. 53.
55 Ibid., p. 76.
56 Ibid., p. 162.
57 Ibid., pp. 133–4.

PSYCHIC BLINDNESS: HATING

1 Bruno Bettelheim, cited in Elisabeth Badinter, *The Conflict: How
   Modern Motherhood Undermines the Status of Women*, trans. Adriana
   Hunter (New York: Metropolitan Books, 2012), p. 45.
2 Nina Sutton, *Bruno Bettelheim: The Other Side of Madness* (London:
   Duckworth, 1995).
3 D. W. Winnicott, 'Hate in the Counter-Transference', *International
   Journal of Psychoanalysis*, 30:2, 1949, p. 73 (also in *Through
   Paediatrics to Psychoanalysis: Collected Papers of D. W. Winnicott*,
   London: Routledge, 1992).
4 Ibid., p. 74.
5 Ibid.
6 Ibid.
7 Ibid.
8 Daisy Waugh, *I Don't Know Why She Bothers: Guilt-Free Motherhood
   for Thoroughly Modern Women* (London: Weidenfeld & Nicolson,
   2013), p. 14.
9 Alison Bechdel, *Are You My Mother? A Comic Drama* (London:
   Jonathan Cape, 2012), p. 21.
10 Winnicott, p. 72.
11 Adrienne Rich, *Of Woman Born: Motherhood as Experience and
   Institution* (New York: Norton, 1976, 1995), p. xxxiii.
12 Bechdel, p. 258.
13 Ibid., p. 178.
14 Ibid., p. 68.

15 Ibid., p. 172.

16 Ibid., p. 65.

17 Sylvia Plath, *Three Women – A Poem for Three Voices*, 1962, in *Collected Poems* (London: Faber, 1981).

18 Ibid., p. 181, p. 186, pp. 180–1.

19 Ibid., p. 181.

20 Sylvia Plath to Aurelia Plath, 21 and 25 October 1962, in *Letters Home: Correspondence 1950–1963*, selected and edited with commentary by Aurelia Schober Plath (London: Faber, 1975), p. 473, p. 477.

21 Melanie Klein, 'Some Reflections on *The Oresteia*', in *Envy and Gratitude and Other Works, 1946–1963* (London: Hogarth Press, 1975), p. 299.

22 All quotes from W. R. Bion, 'Container and Contained', 1962, in *Attention and Interpretation* (London: Karnac, 1970), p. 72, p. 78.

23 Melissa Benn, *Madonna and Child: Towards a New Politics of Motherhood* (London: Jonathan Cape, 1998), p. 21.

24 Estela Welldon, *Mother, Madonna, Whore: The Idealization and Denigration of Motherhood* (London: Karnac, 1988), pp. 78–9.

25 Brid Featherstone, '"I wouldn't do your job!" Women, Social Work and Child Abuse', in *Mothering and Ambivalence*, ed. Wendy Hollway and Brid Featherstone (New York: Routledge, 1997), p. 167.

26 Ibid., p. 185.

27 Rich, p. 279.

28 Ibid., p. xxxv.

29 Simone de Beauvoir, *Le Deuxième sexe*, folio II, p. 351, translated and edited by H. M. Parshley, 1953 (London: Vintage, 1997), p. 513 (all translations modified).

30 Ibid.

31 Ibid., folio I, p. 59, p. 112 (trans. p. 55, p. 94).

32 Ibid., p. 93.

33 Ibid., p. 390.

34 Ibid., II, p. 351 (trans. p. 513).

35 Ibid., II, p. 372 (trans. p. 528–529).

36 Ibid., II, p. 349 (trans. p. 512).

37 Ibid., I, p. 93 (trans. p. 82).

38 Ibid., II, p. 381 (trans. p. 354).

39 Ibid., II, p. 385 (trans. p. 537).

40 See Julia Kristeva, *Je me voyage – Mémoires: Entretiens avec Samuel Dock* (Paris: Fayard, 2017) p. 148, p. 157, p. 188. See also Kristeva's extraordinary split-page meditation on classical and religious icons

of maternity alongside her account of the birth of her son, 'Stabat Mater,' 1977, in *The Kristeva Reader*, ed. Toril Moi (Oxford: Blackwell, 1986).

41 Rivka Galchen, *Little Labours* (New York: New Directions, 2016; London: Fourth Estate, 2017), p. 7.

42 Elena Ferrante, *Frantumaglia: A Writer's Journey*, trans. Ann Goldstein (New York: Europa, 2016), p. 65.

THE AGONY AND THE ECSTASY: ELENA FERRANTE

1 Elena Ferrante, *Frantumaglia: A Writer's Journey*, trans. Ann Goldstein (New York: Europa, 2016), p. 252.

2 Ibid., p. 177, p. 252.

3 Ibid., p. 187.

4 Ibid., p. 206.

5 Ibid., p. 188.

6 D. W. Winnicott, 'The Use of an Object and Relating Through Identification', 1968, in *Playing and Reality* (London: Tavistock, 1971); Jessica Benjamin's *The Bonds of Love: Psychoanalysis, Feminism and the Problem of Domination* (New York: Pantheon, London: Virago, 1988) is the classic feminist psychoanalytic text for exploring the agonistic side of the mother–baby interaction.

7 Elena Ferrante, *The Days of Abandonment*, 2002, trans. Ann Goldstein (New York: Europa, 2005), p. 168.

8 Elena Ferrante, *Troubling Love*, 1992, trans. Ann Goldstein (New York: Europa, 2006), p. 113.

9 Ferrante, *Frantumaglia*, p. 17.

10 Ibid., p. 220.

11 Elena Ferrante, *The Lost Daughter*, 2006, trans. Ann Goldstein (New York: Europa, 2008), p. 206.

12 Ferrante, *Frantumaglia*, p. 254, p. 267.

13 Ibid., p. 267.

14 Ferrante, *Lost Daughter*, p. 53.

15 Ferrante, *Frantumaglia*, p. 347, p. 350.

16 Zoe Williams, 'Why baby books make you miserable', *Guardian*, 3 October, 2017.

17 Ferrante, *Frantumaglia*, p. 198.

18 Ibid., p. 220.

19 Ibid., p. 251.

20 Ferrante, *Days of Abandonment*, p. 127.

21 John Bell, Sophie Boyron and Simon Whittaker, *Principles of French*

Law (Oxford: OUP, 2008), p. 264.

22 Elena Ferrante, *Those Who Leave and Those Who Stay – Middle Time*, trans. Ann Goldstein (New York: Europa, 2014), p. 372.

23 Elena Ferrante, *The Story of a New Name – Youth*, trans. Ann Goldstein (New York: Europa, 2013), p. 112.

24 Ferrante, *Lost Daughter*, p. 124.

25 Ferrante, *Story of a New Name*, p. 311.

26 Ibid.

27 Ibid., p. 91.

28 Ferrante, *Lost Daughter*, p. 87.

29 Ibid., p. 37, p. 23.

30 Ibid., p. 122.

31 Elena Ferrante, *My Brilliant Friend – Childhood, Adolescence*, trans. Ann Goldstein (New York: Europa, 2012), p. 322.

32 Ferrante, *Those Who Leave and Those Who Stay*, p. 76.

33 Elena Ferrante, *The Story of the Lost Child – Maturity, Old Age*, trans. Ann Goldstein (New York: Europa, 2015), p. 151.

34 Ibid., p. 208.

35 Ferrante, *Troubling Love*, p. 87.

36 Ibid., p 139.

37 Ferrante, *Frantumaglia*, p. 122, p. 140.

38 Ibid., p. 326.

39 Ibid.

40 Ibid., p. 277.

41 Ibid., p. 379.

42 Ibid., p. 380.

43 Ibid., p. 224.

44 Ibid., p. 221.

45 Ibid., p. 222.

46 Ferrante, *Lost Daughter*, p. 124, p. 122.

47 Ferrante, *Story of a New Name*, p. 113.

48 Ferrante, *Those Who Leave and Those Who Stay*, p. 233.

49 Ibid., *Story of a New Name*, p. 378.

50 Ferrante, *Those Who Leave and Those Who Stay*, p. 238.

51 Ferrante, *Frantumaglia*, p. 116.

52 Ibid., p. 98.

53 Ibid., p. 223.

54 Lucy Jones, 'As she is born, part of me is dying', *Guardian*, 9 January 2017.

55 Ferrante, *Story of a New Name*, p. 372.

56 Ferrante, *Lost Daughter*, p. 125.
57 Ferrante, *Frantumaglia*, p. 222.
58 Ibid., p. 193.
59 Ibid., p. 99.
60 Ibid.
61 Ibid.
62 Ferrante, *My Brilliant Friend*, p. 229.
63 Ferrante, *Frantumaglia*, p. 239.
64 Ibid., p. 100.
65 Ibid.
66 Ibid.
67 Ibid., p. 176, *Story of the Lost Child*, p. 175.
68 Ferrante, *Story of a New Name*, p. 289.
69 Ibid.
70 Ferrante, *Story of the Lost Child*, p. 466.
71 Ferrante, *My Brilliant Friend*, p. 231.
72 William Maxwell, *They Came Like Swallows*, 1937, London: Vintage, 2008, p. 10.
73 Ibid.
74 Ibid., p. 11, pp. 31–2.
75 Ferrante, *Frantumaglia*, p. 146.
76 Ibid., p. 367.
77 Ibid., p. 147.
78 Ferrante, *Story of the Lost Child*, p. 309.
79 Ferrante, *Those Who Leave and Those Who Stay*, p. 290.
80 Ibid., p. 291 (emphasis original).
81 Ibid.
82 Ferrante, *Frantumaglia*, p. 368 (emphasis original).
83 Ibid., p. 54.
84 Ibid., p. 220.
85 Ibid., p. 66.
86 Ibid., p. 90.
87 Ibid., p. 92.
88 Ibid., p. 201.
89 Ferrante, *Those Who Leave and Those Who Stay*, p. 28.
90 Ferrante, *Frantumaglia*, p. 336.
91 Ibid., p. 217.
92 Ibid., p. 368.
93 Ibid., p. 268, p. 326.
94 Ibid.

95 Ibid., p. 301, p. 286.

96 Ibid., p. 126.

97 Ibid., pp. 126–7.

98 Ferrante, *Days of Abandonment*, p. 127.

99 Ibid., p. 224.

100 Ferrante, *Frantumaglia*, p. 347, p. 350.

THE AGONY AND THE ECSTASY: INSIDE OUT

1   Sylvia Plath, 'Morning Song', in *Ariel* (London: Faber, 1965).

2   Marjorie Perloff, 'The Two Ariels: The (Re)making of the Sylvia Plath Canon', *American Poetry Review*, November–December 1984.

3   Danuta Kean, 'Plath accused Hughes of beating her and wanting her dead, trove of letters shows', *Guardian*, 11 April 2017.

4   Darian Leader, *Strictly Bipolar* (London: Penguin, 2013).

5   Fiona Shaw, *Out of Me: The Story of a Postnatal Breakdown* (London: Penguin, 1997).

6   Lou-Marie Kruger, Kirsten van Straaten, Laura Taylor, Marleen Lourens and Carla Dukas, 'The Melancholy of Murderous Mothers: Depression and the Medicalization of Women's Anger', *Feminism and Psychology*, published online, 30 June 2014, p. 8. My thanks to Lou-Marie Kruger for bringing this work to my attention.

7   Ibid.

8   Virginia Woolf, *The Years*, 1937 (Oxford: OUP, 1992), p. 359 (emphasis mine).

9   Linda Kerber, 'The Republican Mother: Women and the Enlightenment – An American Perspective', *American Quarterly*, 28:2, 1976, cited in Shaul Bar-Haim, *The Maternalizing Movement: Psychoanalysis, Motherhood and the British Welfare State c. 1920–1950*, unpublished PhD thesis, Birkbeck 2015, p. 18.

10 Sigmund Freud, 'The Disillusionment of the War', in *Thoughts for the Times on War and Death*, 1915, Standard Edn, vol.14 (London: Hogarth Press, 1957), p. 276; *The Future of an Illusion*, Standard Edn, vol. 21 (London: Hogarth Press, 1961), p. 20.

11 Freud, *The Future of an Illusion*, p. 12.

12 My thanks to Miranda Carter for alerting me to this series, and to Margaret and Lucy Reynolds for the occasion we watched it together.

13 Buchi Emecheta, *The Joys of Motherhood* (Oxford: Heinemann, 1979).

14 For a sustained, political critique of the concept of happiness, see Sara Ahmed, *The Promise of Happiness* (Durham: Duke University Press, 2010).

15 Simon de Beauvoir, *Le Deuxième sexe*, folio II, p. 385 (trans. p. 537).

16 Elena Ferrante, *Frantumaglia: A Writer's Journey*, trans. Ann Goldstein (New York: Europa, 2016), p. 100.

17 Susan Stryker, 'My Words to Victor Frankenstein Above the Village of Chamounix', *GLQ: A Journal of Lesbian and Gay Studies*, 1:3, 1994.

18 Ibid.

19 Ibid.

20 Ibid.

21 Sindiwe Magona, *Mother to Mother* (Claremont: David Philip, and Boston: Beacon Press, 1998), p. 127.

22 Ibid., p. 2.

23 Ibid., p. 210.

24 Ibid., p. 185.

25 Ibid., p. 201.

26 Ibid., p. 198.

27 Amy Biehl's parents, Linda and Peter Biehl, befriended the man convicted of her murder, after he was released from prison, and two other men who were in the crowd, employing them at the charitable foundation they established in her memory. For one version of this story see Justine van der Leun, *We Are Not Such Things: A Murder in a South African Township and the Search for Truth and Reconciliation* (London: 4th Estate, 2016). See also Gillian Slovo's critique of the book, 'The Politics of Forgiveness', *Literary Review*, 445, August 2016.

PERMISSIONS CREDITS

Page vii: Quotations from *The Return* (2016) by Hisham Matar and from *Autumn* (2016) by Ali Smith are included with the kind permission of the authors.

Page 90: Quotations from song lyrics by Hole:

'Plump' written by Eric Erlandson and Courtney Love
© Published by Mother May I Music
Administered by Kobalt Music Publishing Ltd

'Softer, Softest' written by Eric Erlandson and Courtney Love
© Published by Mother May I Music
Administered by Kobalt Music Publishing Ltd

'I Think That I Would Die' written by Eric Erlandson and Courtney Love
© Published by Mother May I Music
Administered by Kobalt Music Publishing Ltd

Pages 122–3: Quotations from 'Three Women: A Poem for Three Voices' by Sylvia Plath, taken from *Winter Trees*

INDEX